Dave,

We hope this book can give you some measure of comfort that God loves you and He is with you every step of the way.

    May God bless you and heal your heart.

        Love
           Keven & Claire
             Baxter

HOPE FOR
Hurting
HEARTS

GREG LAURIE

Hope for Hurting Hearts

Unless otherwise indicated, all Scripture quotations are taken from: The Holy Bible, New King James Version © 1984 by Thomas Nelson, Inc.

Scripture quotations marked (NIV) are from The Holy Bible, New International Version®, NIV®. Copyright © 1973, 1978, 1984 by International Bible Society. Used by permission of Zondervan Publishing House. Scripture quotations marked (TLB) are taken from The Living Bible, copyright © 1971 by Tyndale House Publishers, Wheaton, Illinois. Scripture quotations marked (NLT) are taken from The New Living Translation, copyright © 1996, 2004 by Tyndale Charitable Trust. Used by permission of Tyndale House Publishers. All rights reserved. Scripture quotations marked (THE MESSAGE) are taken from The Message, by Eugene Peterson. Copyright © 1993, 1994, 1995, 1996, 2000, 2001, 2002. Used by permission of NavPress Publishing Group. All rights reserved. Scripture quotations marked (PHILLIPS) are from The New Testament in Modern English, Revised Edition © 1958, 1960, 1972 by J. B. Phillips.

ISBN 0-9843327-9-3

Printed in the United States of America.

Published by: Kerygma Publishing–Dana Point, California
Coordination: FM Management, Ltd.
Cover Design: Ross Geerdes
Cover Photography: Trever Hoehne
Interior Design, Production: Highgate Cross+Cathey, Ltd.

Contents

◈ ONE ◈
Where Were You, Lord?

Have you ever had a crisis overwhelm you—maybe even to the point where you didn't think you could survive the experience? Have you ever found yourself facing a set of circumstances so crushing, so utterly devastating that you couldn't imagine how you could ever get through? Have you ever wondered why God allowed a tragedy in your life or in the life of someone close to you?

Perhaps you found yourself saying, in so many words, *"Lord, where were You?"*

In the New Testament book of John, the Bible gives us a true-life account of two sisters who had to wrestle with all of those questions. It's the story of an unexpected death, and how it brought a great trial of faith and shattered the happiness of a close-knit little family.

But it is also the story of how Jesus responds to such situations—and how God can gain glory through it all.

This story resonates with me in a deep and highly personal way, because on July 24, 2008, at 9:05 in the morning, our son Christopher's earthly life came to a sudden and unexpected end in an automobile accident in Southern California.

Christopher Laurie was only thirty-three years old, and had been walking with the Lord when he departed for heaven so quickly. He had a wife, Brittany, a toddler—our precious granddaughter, Stella—with another baby on the way. He was working at our church, Harvest Christian Fellowship, doing graphic design, growing in his walk with Christ, and studying the Bible more than at any other time in his life. In fact, he had only recently opened up his home for a small group Bible study. We were so proud of Christopher and Brittany's progress in the Lord, and how He was blessing them.

But just because you're serving the Lord doesn't mean you'll avoid tests, trials, and tragedy in your life. Far from it! Satan, our determined enemy in the Christian life, will look for every opportunity to trip us up—whether through direct attack or little harassments from whatever angle he can manage. Christopher had been going through a few such trials this past summer, not long before his accident, so I had sent an e-mail to him with these words:

Christopher,

You are doing the Lord's work now, and the devil will attack you in strange ways. But think about it. You are doing cutting-edge graphics that are helping to get the gospel out around the world. You are involved in a home Bible study that is touching your friends and family. You are realizing your God-given potential. And you know what? Better things are coming! God has blessed you and the enemy will simply attack. So keep doing what you are doing. That's what I always have done. When attack comes, I "batten down the hatches" and go at it even harder, because I know the enemy's objective is to distract and discourage me. When Nehemiah was building the walls of Jerusalem, he came under criticism and attack for it. So you know what he did? He just kept building that wall. And that's what you need to do, too. Mom and I love you very much, and we are proud of you and Brittany. P.S. We like Stella quite a bit, too!

We knew he would appreciate the humor of that last line, because we are just head over heels in love with little Stella. So Christopher wrote me back.

Dad,

Thank you so much for your loving encouragement. I am so thankful for what the Lord has done in my life the last couple years. I want what He wants for me. I have been blessed with the most wealth I have ever wanted: loving parents and a brother who serves the Lord and desires Him first, a beautiful wife who knows Jesus, a beautiful daughter with another on the way. I am truly rich and no man can take those things from me. I love you and mom so very much. Please be safe in your travels, talk to you soon.

Love, tof.

Tof, or Topher was his nickname. (Short for Christopher.)

My son had been excited about working on a documentary film called *Lost Boy* (that also came out in book form), which tells the story of my turbulent growing up years, how God intervened in my life, and how I came to faith in Jesus Christ. Christopher had done all the graphics for the film, and had responsibility for the art direction. I had waited a long time to tell that story, but finally felt like it was the right time. Looking back on my childhood and early years, I felt that the ink had dried, so to speak, and that I could now objectively tell the story. Mostly, I wanted to express the message, "Here is how God can bring good out of bad."

I had survived a crazy childhood, growing up in an alcoholic home, with my mom being married and divorced seven times. But I came to Christ in high school, at the age of seventeen, and turned my life over to the Lord.

The stats all say that if you come from a divorced home, you will most likely end up divorced yourself. But by God's grace and against all odds, my wife and I just celebrated our thirty-fifth wedding anniversary. So all in all, in spite of the heartbreaks in those early days, it's been a pretty happy story. The film closes with our family walking down the street together, and it's almost as though you could write the words on the screen: "And they lived happily ever after" at the end of the story.

I had been showing this film in various churches in different parts of the country, and I would speak afterwards, telling the biblical story of Joseph, how he faced many adverse circumstances in his life, and how God brought good results out of evil circumstances. Not that bad is good, but God can bring good *out of* bad, and bring glory to His great name through it all.

And then came that morning in July when we got the terrible, incomprehensible news about Christopher.

Good out of bad? The best results out of the worst circumstances? Was the message of "Lost Boy"—or more importantly, of the Bible itself—still true, or was it all a sham?

Even in the depths of our grieving, we had to say, yes, the message of that movie and book—or more to the point, my life story—hadn't changed. The chronicle of God's grace and faithfulness that we told in *Lost Boy* is as true as ever. It's just that we find ourselves in the midst of a life chapter we would have never, never chosen. God will still bring good out of bad, and bring glory to Himself. But at this writing, the sorrow is still fresh in our hearts. We still have a lot of grieving—and healing—to do.

And so it was for that loving little family in the town of Bethany, just a short walk from Jerusalem. In John 11, the Bible gives us the story of three siblings, Mary, Martha, and Lazarus, and the tragedy that came into their lives.

What makes this story especially interesting is this family's close friendship with the controversial young rabbi, named Jesus. Mary, Martha, and Lazarus happened to be intimate friends of Jesus during His three-year ministry.

When Jesus visited Jerusalem, He liked to spend time (and enjoy the hospitality) of His good friends. Mary honored the Lord and showed her devotion by wiping His feet with a special perfume. Martha demonstrated her love by preparing delicious meals for Jesus and His men. And Lazarus was always there—a warm and welcoming friend.

Jesus would frequent their home, evidently enjoying the companionship and the refuge from the suspicion and hostility He so often encountered in Jerusalem. Think of it! These were three people who honestly counted Jesus Christ as close personal friends. But one day while Jesus was in another part of the country, Lazarus became very ill. Mary and Martha did all they could for their brother, and then did what every person ought to do in a time of crisis. They sent word to Jesus to ask for His help.

That is where the story begins.

> Now a certain man was sick, Lazarus of Bethany, the town of Mary and her sister Martha. It was that Mary who anointed the Lord with fragrant oil and wiped His feet with her hair, whose brother Lazarus was sick. Therefore the sisters sent to Him, saying, "Lord, behold, he whom You love is sick." (John 11:1-3)

So what do we learn from this little introduction to the story?

#1: This life will have its sorrows

Having a close relationship with Jesus did not mean that Mary, Martha and Lazarus would be exempt from suffering. In our lives here on earth, we will experience pain, grief, sickness, and the death of loved ones. I know that is a sobering point, but it's true, and we might just as well come to grips with it and stop running from it.

When you're younger, you don't necessarily understand this. As you get older, however, you usually experience the death of your grandparents first. And then as time passes, your parents will die. As you continue to age, your spouse may pass on before you, and you know that day will eventually come for you, too, and your children will bury you.

Hard as those realities may be to deal with, there are situations that are even more difficult still. And those are the unexpected deaths that we encounter in the course of our lives. It might be the death of a spouse, an infant, a teenager, a sibling, or someone that is close to us in age. And suddenly we are made aware of our own mortality as well as the ones we love so deeply.

That was the case with Mary, Martha, and Lazarus. They were a tight, loving little family, and then suddenly one of them was at the point of death. But ironically, it was through this experience that they learned even more about the power and love of Jesus Christ.

Yes, life certainly has its sorrows. But there is a second point that overwhelms even this reality.

#2: God loves us

Don't rush past those words. Let them sink in. *God loves you.* Truly. Deeply. Eternally. God will never allow anything to happen in your life as His child that is not motivated by His everlasting love for you. In Jeremiah 31:3, God says, "I have loved you with an everlasting love;

therefore with lovingkindness I have drawn you."

Mary and Martha knew this. In fact, they were sure of it. They knew Jesus loved each member of their family. And take note of the way they appealed to Jesus in this crisis. They didn't say, "Lord, the one that is devoted to You is sick." Or even, "The one that loves You is sick." But rather they said, "The one that *You love* is sick."

That's a good thing to remember when we make our appeal to God. Never appeal on the basis of your own devotion.

> *"Lord Your great servant is calling upon You now."*
> No. Because I am not a great servant.
> *"Lord the one that loves You so passionately is asking for help now."*
> No. Because my love is fickle and inconsistent.
> *"Lord, the one the You love is in need."*

That ought to be our approach, for He has declared His love for us over and over again. Notice, they didn't even tell Him what to do. They didn't say, "Drop whatever You're doing, rush home to us, and do something now." They just said, in effect, "We wanted to let You know, because we believe You will know exactly what to do."

But here is something interesting. When they use the word love in their message to the Lord, it's the Greek term *phileo*—a word that means "brother" or "friendship" love. It's as though they were saying, "Lord, Your friend, Your buddy, Your companion, isn't feeling well. In fact, He is terribly ill. So please do something."

But then we encounter verses 4 through 6:

> When Jesus heard that, He said, "This sickness is not
> unto death, but for the glory of God, that the Son of
> God may be glorified through it." Now Jesus loved
> Martha and her sister and Lazarus. So, when He heard
> that he was sick, He stayed two more days in the place
> where He was."

The word John used to describe the love of Jesus for
Lazarus is the Greek word *agape*. It is not "brother love."
It is a different kind of love. It is God's supernatural, all-
consuming love.

So effectively, what this is saying to us is that God's
love for us may be demonstrated in ways we won't always
understand. At first glance, this story really doesn't make
sense. The Bible tells us that Jesus *loved* Lazarus—loved
him deeply, with a love that goes far beyond earthly, broth-
erly love and affection. Yet when Lazarus was in the hour
of his deepest crisis, Jesus chose to delay His response. He
had the power to heal His friend, but withheld that power.
He could have come sooner, but He didn't. Why would He
do that?

Because Jesus wanted to do more than they were expecting.

You and I live in the here-and-now. That's all we know.
God, however, lives in the here-and-now and in the eternal.
As mortal human beings, creatures of flesh and blood, we
tend to be consumed with those things that will benefit

us right now. In other words, what will make my life a little bit more comfortable? What will make me a little bit happier or more fulfilled? God, however, always looks at the big picture. His thoughts include questions like these: "What can I do to make you more like Jesus? What can I do to conform you more into My image? How can I transform you and make you stronger spiritually?" We will always ask Him for certain things that seem to work within our lives as we know them. But God sees far beyond what we see, and knows our needs better than we know them ourselves.

Paul tells us "For our present troubles are quite small and won't last very long. Yet they produce for us an immeasurably great glory that will last forever!" (2 Corinthians 4:17, NLT)

That's exactly what was happening in this story. Yes, Jesus certainly loved Lazarus—and his sisters. But He was planning to demonstrate this in a different way than they could have ever imagined. And He began by completely mystifying them, as He deliberately delayed His arrival.

By the time He set out for Bethany, the issue had already been settled. Or so it seemed.

> Then after this He said to the disciples, "Let us go to Judea again…. Our friend Lazarus sleeps, but I go that I may wake him up." Then His disciples said, "Lord, if he sleeps he will get well." However, Jesus spoke of his death, but they thought that He was speaking about taking rest in sleep. Then Jesus said to them plainly, "Lazarus is dead. And I am glad for your sakes that I

was not there, that you may believe. Nevertheless let us go to him." (vv. 7, 11-15)

Not only had Lazarus passed on, he had already been dead and buried for four days. So there was no bringing him back. He was long gone. And that was when Jesus arrived back in town.

Martha, hearing that Jesus was on His way, went to meet Him.

> Then Martha, as soon as she heard that Jesus was coming, went and met Him, but Mary was sitting in the house. Now Martha said to Jesus, "Lord, if You had been here, my brother would not have died. But even now I know that whatever You ask of God, God will give You." Jesus said, 'Your brother will rise again.' Martha said to Him, "I know that he will rise again in the resurrection at the last day." Jesus said to her, "I am the resurrection and the life. He who believes in Me, though he may die, he shall live. And whoever lives and believes in Me shall never die. Do you believe this?" She said to Him, "Yes, Lord, I believe that You are the Christ, the Son of God, who is to come into the world." And when she had said these things, she went her way and secretly called Mary her sister, saying, "The Teacher has come and is calling for you." (vv. 20-28)

Martha was never one to hold her tongue. You always knew where you stood with this lady! "Lord," she said, "if You would have been here my brother would not have died." To paraphrase it, *"Where were You anyway, Jesus?"*

Maybe you've said something similar during or after some crisis in your life.

> *"Lord, where were You when my parents divorced?"*
> *"Lord, where were You when we got that diagnosis of cancer?"*
> *"Lord, where were You when our marriage fell apart?"*
> *"Lord, where were You when I lost my job?"*
> *"Lord, where were You when my child got in trouble?"*
> *"Lord, where were You when my loved one died?"*

I want you to notice something very important here. Jesus did not reprove Martha for what she said. Why do I bring this up? Because you need to know that it's not wrong to tell God exactly how you feel. I think sometimes we get the idea that it's irreverent or even sinful to express our real fears or the doubts of our heart, even to God.

But Martha didn't hold back.

And Jesus didn't condemn her for it.

When we read the psalms, we learn that there were many times when David and the other psalmists really "let down their hair" with God. They cried out to Him, and emptied the contents of their hearts in His presence.

In Psalm 42, the writer says,

> "O God my Rock...why have you forsaken me? Why must I suffer these attacks from my enemies?" Their taunts pierce me like a fatal wound; again and again they scoff, "Where is that God of yours?" (vv. 9-10, TLB)

So the psalmist is saying, "Lord, from where I sit right now, it sure seems to me like You've forsaken me... Like You're not even paying attention to me." And then he corrects himself and says in verse 11 of the same psalm, "But, O my soul, don't be discouraged. Don't be upset. Expect God to act! For I know that I shall again have plenty of reason to praise Him for all that He will do. He is my help! He is my God!"

I have done this many times. In my pain, I will cry out to God. I won't tell you what I say, because that's between God and myself. But sometimes the reality that my son is gone pierces my heart like a sword , and I say, "Oh, God. I can't believe this! I can't handle this pain!" But then I will preach to myself and I will say, "Now, Greg listen to me. Your son is alive in the presence of the Lord, and you are going to see him again before you know it in heaven." And I will remind myself of the promises of God.

My prayers, however, are wide open and honest. I pour out my heart before God, describing my pain to Him. But I also remind myself of God's truth. And this is what prayer is.

God wants us to cry out to Him.

He invites us to pour out our hearts before Him. David writes:

> Trust in him at all times, O people;
> pour out your hearts to him,
> for God is our refuge (Psalm 62:8, NIV).

Even Jesus hanging on the cross cried out, "My God, My God, why have You forsaken me." Even as He was bearing the sins of the world, He cried out to His Father.

In the same way, even in our worst pain, we should cry out to God.

David said, "Trust in Him at all times—pour out your hearts to Him and take refuge in Him." Sometimes, you and I don't do that. Sometimes we allow trouble and trauma and hardship to cause us to be angry with God, so that we withdraw from Him and don't want to talk to Him.

No, my friend, that's when you need Him more than ever! Cry out to Him with your doubts. Cry out to Him with your pain. He will patiently, lovingly, hear you. He might set your crooked thinking straight as you seek Him, but He wants you to pour out your pain. He loves you!

As one paraphrase of Psalm 55:22 puts it: "Pile your troubles on God's shoulders—he'll carry your load, he'll help you out."[1]

Think about Job, and the way he responded to devastating circumstances. Talk about having your life fall apart! Job not only lost a son, he lost *seven sons and three daughters* in one unimaginable day. And that was in addition to losing all his possessions and his health! But what did Job do? The Bible says he did not charge God foolishly. Instead, he cried out to the Lord, "Naked I came from my mother's womb, and naked shall I return there. The LORD gave, and the LORD has taken away; blessed be the name of the LORD" (Job 1:21).

In fairness, Job did go on to question God in the days to come, saying, "Lord why?" There's nothing wrong with asking God why, as long as you don't get the idea that He somehow owes you an answer. Frankly God doesn't owe you or me an explanation.

Concerning our recent tragedy, I too have asked "why?" Why did this happen? Why couldn't it have been me instead of him? I'm fifty-six. He's thirty-three. I've lived enough life. Christopher was a loving husband, father, brother, and friend to many. He was walking with and serving God. Why did the Lord take him? I have many such questions roiling in my heart.

I was speaking with Pastor Chuck Smith about this and he made this statement to me: "Never trade what you don't know for what you do know." Those words stopped me in my tracks a little. I asked myself, "Well, what do I know for sure?"

> *I know that God loves me.*
> *I know that God loves my wife and other son, Jonathan.*
> *I know that God loved and loves my son, Christopher.*
> *I know that God loves Brittany and Stella and the daughter Christopher never met.*
> *I know that Christopher is well and alive in the best place he could ever be.*
> *I know that God can make good things come out of bad.*
> *I know that we'll all be together again—not so very long from now—on in heaven.*

I KNOW those things. I'm a sure as I can be. So I'm making the choice to stand on what I know instead of what I don't know.

So if you were to ask me, "Greg, why did this happen?" My answer is, "I don't know. And I don't know that I will ever know. I just know that I need God more than I have ever needed Him in my life."

The old hymn states, "I need Thee every hour." For me, that is literally true. I do need Him every hour, and I need Him desperately. In fact, I need him every sixty seconds. In times of deep sorrow I will sometimes call out my son's name, "Christopher!" Then I say, "Jesus!" I have never been so conscious of my utter dependence upon the Lord, just to make it through my days. And that is a fact that is both heartbreaking and wonderful.

And what about the days ahead? In his insightful commentary on the book of Job, Chuck Swindoll writes: "God never promised He would inform us about His plan ahead of time. He just promised He has one. Ultimately it is for our good and His glory. He knows and we don't. That is we shrug and say, 'I don't know.' But I do know this: The death of His Son was not in vain. Christ died for you. And if you believe in Him He will forgive your sins and you will go to live with Him forever. You will have heaven and all the blessings of it. I know that. It is a tough journey getting there. Full of confusion and struggles, shrugs, followed by a lot of 'I don't knows.' But when the heavens open and we are there, there will be no more shrugs, and we will be able to say, 'Now I know.'"[2]

The Bible says that "the secret things belong to the Lord."[3] If God explained to us everything we wanted to know, it still wouldn't satisfy our hearts. His answers would only raise more and more questions. In the end, we don't need His answers as much as we need Him. His presence. His peace. Philippians 4:7 tells us about His peace that surpasses, or transcends, understanding. One translation calls it a "peace which is far more wonderful than the human mind can understand."[4]

It is not necessarily a peace that gives understanding but rather one that *transcends* understanding.

So there are innumerable things we could ask God as to why this happened or that happened. But the bottom line is simply this: Our lives are in His hands, and we must trust Him.

Back in our story about Mary and Martha, obviously Martha was baffled, frustrated, and hurt by Jesus' choice to not come heal her brother. So the Lord tries to help her get an eternal perspective.

> Jesus said to her, "Your brother will rise again."
>
> Martha said to Him, "I know that he will rise again in the resurrection at the last day."
>
> Jesus said to her, "I am the resurrection and the life. He who believes in Me, though he may die, he shall live. And whoever lives and believes in Me shall never die. Do you believe this?"

She said to Him, "Yes, Lord, I believe that You are the Christ, the Son of God, who is to come into the world." (John 11:23-27)

In other words, Jesus was saying to His grieving friend, "Martha, listen to Me. Death is not the end! You're acting as though it's over with. It's *not* over with." And at this point, I think He was speaking of something greater and more profound than even the resurrection of Lazarus, which He would accomplish within that very hour. After all, raising Lazarus from the dead—exciting and joyful as that may have been—was only a temporary proposition! Lazarus would just have to die again in a few years! Isn't it bad enough to die once? Poor Lazarus had to die twice! So I don't think the essential message of the Lord's statement is, "I'm going to raise your brother up from the dead." I think the bigger message was this: "Death is not the end. This is temporary. One day I will get rid of death altogether, and whoever believes in Me will live forever."

Following the Lord's encounter with Martha, her sister Mary comes to greet Jesus.

> Then, when Mary came where Jesus was, and saw Him, she fell down at His feet, saying to Him, "Lord, if You had been here, my brother would not have died."
>
> Therefore, when Jesus saw her weeping, and the Jews who came with her weeping, He groaned in the spirit and was troubled. And He said, "Where have you laid him?"

They said to Him, "Lord, come and see."

Jesus wept. Then the Jews said, "See how He loved him!" (vv. 32-36)

#3: Jesus weeps in our times of pain

Yes, Jesus is God, with all of the attributes that we attribute to Deity. But let's not miss the fact that He is also a man who feels our pains and our sorrows. Isaiah 53 reminds us, "He was despised and rejected—a man of sorrows, acquainted with deepest grief." The passage goes on to say, "Yet it was our weaknesses he carried; it was our sorrows that weighed him down."[5]

He not only carried your sin, He carried your *sorrow*. We're told in Psalm 56:8, "You have seen me tossing and turning through the night. You have collected all my tears and preserved them in your bottle! You have recorded every one in your book" (TLB).

We recently led a tour through Israel with people from our church and our radio audience. I had the opportunity to take my whole family with me, and it was a wonderful trip—the best ever. One day Christopher, Jonathan, and I were exploring the old city of Jerusalem. We were taking photographs, with the idea of eventually putting together a calendar.

At one point in our ramblings, we stopped at an antiquities store, a shop that sells relics from the past. As we looking around, I noticed a number of little bottles in various sizes and shapes. So I asked the shopkeeper, "Sir, what are these bottles for?"

"Oh," he said, "those are Roman tear bottles."

That piqued my curiosity. "What were they used for?" I asked.

"Well, the Romans believed that when a loved one dies, you need to keep your tears in a bottle. So they would store the tears in these little containers."

It's the same concept as David's words in Psalm 56:8.

I have a tear bottle now. But it's not one on earth. It's in heaven. And I'm not the one who has to collect my own tears, because God has already said He would do that. Truthfully, I probably have more than one bottle over on the Other Side, because I have never wept so much in my life. My wife told me recently that she had only seen me cry two or three times in all our years together—and now I can't seem to make it through a day without crying.

So why does God keep our tears in a bottle? Because He sees and cares about every one of them. He takes note of our every tear. He hears our every sigh.

As a friend of mine, Tommy Walker wrote in his song by the title, "He Knows My Name":

> *He knows my name.*
> *He hears me when I call.*
> *He knows each tear that falls.*
> *And He hears me when I call.* [6]

And the Bible says that a day is coming when God will wipe away all of the tears from all of our years from our eyes.

And I heard a loud voice from the throne saying, "Now
the dwelling of God is with men, and he will live with
them. They will be his people, and God himself will be
with them and be their God. He will wipe every tear
from their eyes. There will be no more death or mourning or crying or pain, for the old order of things has
passed away." (Revelation 21:3-4, NIV)

Jesus wept at the death of His friend and the sorrow of
Lazarus's two grieving sisters. And when you find yourself
going through deep waters and times of disappointment
and grief, He weeps with you, too. He cares about you. If it
hurts you, it hurts Him. If it brings sorrow to you, it brings
sorrow to Him.

But the death of His friend also brought Him anger.

Verse 33 tells us: "Therefore, when Jesus saw her weeping, and the Jews who came with her weeping, He groaned
in the spirit and was troubled."

The Greek word used for "troubled" here could be
translated *angry*. Why was Jesus angry? Was He angry
with Mary and Martha for not believing? I don't think so.
Was He angry with the people who had come to comfort
the family, and were mourning the death of Lazarus?
No. I think Jesus was angry at death itself. He was mad at
the grim reaper, if you will. Why? Because this was never
God's plan. God's plan was to have us live forever. God's
plan was that these bodies would never age or wear out or
experience sickness or limitations.

So He was angry over that, and wept over that. But

these weren't tears of "frustration." God is never frustrated. Jesus was angry and then did something about it that had been planned from eternity past. He gave up His life on a Roman cross, dying for the sins of the world, and then raising again from the dead. And the Bible says He has become the "firstfruits" of those that sleep, which means He went before us.[7]

And because He went before us into death and came out victorious on the other side, those of us who now live and face death can be confident and unafraid.

Death is not the end.

Life, in another form and in another place, goes on.

So what should our response to these things be? We are to honor and glorify God.

#4: God can be glorified through human suffering

Then Jesus, again groaning in Himself, came to the tomb. It was a cave, and a stone lay against it. Jesus said, "Take away the stone."

Martha, the sister of him who was dead, said to Him, "Lord, by this time there is a stench, for he has been dead four days."

Jesus said to her, "Did I not say to you that if you would believe you would see the glory of God?" Then they took away the stone from the place where the dead man was lying. And Jesus lifted up His eyes and said, "Father, I thank You that You have heard Me. And I know that You always hear Me, but because of the people who are standing by I said this, that they may believe that You sent Me." Now when He had said these things, He cried with a loud voice, "Lazarus, come forth!" And he who had died came out bound hand and foot with graveclothes, and his face was wrapped with a cloth. Jesus said to them, "Loose him, and let him go." (vv. 38-44)

It was a great miracle…one of the greatest in the New Testament. And to this very day, God will work just that way at certain times and in certain places; He will step into your life and dramatically, miraculously, change your circumstances. You will go to the doctor, and hear Him say, "I'm really sorry. There's nothing we can do for you. You'd better just get your affairs in order, because you only have a short time to live." But you cry out to the Lord to do that which only He can do, and He does a miracle and heals you. He steps into your adverse circumstances and intervenes.

What do we do in a situation like that? We glorify the Lord. And sometimes that's the way He gains glory, by completely removing the difficulty from us. There's nothing wrong with calling out to Him and asking Him for that.

But that's not the only way He is glorified. Sometimes God is glorified *through* the adversity.

The apostle Paul, an amazingly tough guy by anyone's definition, had his own issues with suffering. There was one particular physical condition afflicting him that had Paul so distressed, so troubled, that he cried out to God for relief. Here is how he explained it to the believers in Corinth:

> I was given a physical handicap—one of Satan's angels—to harass me.... Three times I begged the Lord for it to leave me, but his reply has been, "My grace is enough for you: for where there is weakness, my power is shown the more completely." Therefore, I have cheerfully made up my mind to be proud of my weaknesses, because they mean a deeper experience of the power of Christ. I can even enjoy weaknesses, suffering, privations, persecutions and difficulties for Christ's sake. For my very weakness makes me strong in him.
> (2 Corinthians 12:7-10, Phillips)

In effect, Paul concluded: "All right, if God says I am to endure this, then that's what I'll do. If it's all for Christ's good, and part of His good plan, then I'll be content with whatever He chooses to give me."

Suffering can strengthen us, if we let it. It can make us more like the Lord. When a Christian suffers and gives glory to God through it all, it reassures the rest of us that there will never be a valley so deep that God will not get us through it.

We may wish we could dodge all the unpleasantness of life on a broken planet, but none of us gets a pass on suffering. Some will suffer more than others. Some will face more calamity and heartache. We know that. But one day, we will all have to face the inevitability of our mortality. We will all experience tragedy in this life, and most of us will know what it means to have a loved one die unexpectedly.

When you see something like that happen in the life of another believer, when you see a Christian suffering through one of these heartbreaking seasons of life and glorifying God through it all, it gives you hope. You say to yourself, "She made it through, so I can, too. He's giving God glory through the worst of it, so I will do that as well."

God can be glorified through the suffering of a Christian, and use it to display His power to a lost world. Unbelievers could look at some of our lives and say, "You Christians talk about your faith, but your lives are pretty good, all things considered."

But what do they say when they see us go through a time of setbacks, injustice, or suffering, and still maintain a sweet spirit and a strong faith in Jesus Christ? Some of these people outside of the faith might very well say, "How do they do that? Could this faith of theirs be genuine? Could there really be something to it?" The trials and hardships give the believer a platform from which they can give witness to their faith in Christ. Why? Because they are actually living it out in the real world.

Think of Corrie ten Boom, who lost her father and sister in a Nazi concentration camp, but survived miraculously herself. She spent the rest of her life telling people that there is no pit so deep that God is not deeper still. And she was able to forgive those who had perpetuated these evils on her family and friends.

Consider Joni Eareckson Tada. Through a freak diving accident at age seventeen, she became a quadriplegic. That was over forty years ago, and in that time she has reached untold multitudes of people from every walk of life around the world with her powerful, positive testimony for Jesus Christ.

Think of Nick Vujicic, who came and spoke at our church, and was born without limbs. We all marveled as we heard his story, and his many opportunities to serve the Lord and speak for Him. You just have to pay attention to a man like that, because he faces what we would call horrendous circumstances every day of his life, and honors God through it all.

WHAT IS "BETTER"?

In my email to my son I concluded by saying, "Better things are coming."

Was I wrong? I don't think so. No, they weren't the "better things" I would have chosen for Christopher, or for his family. I would have chosen a long life for him, and for the privilege of seeing his children and grandchildren grow up and serve the Lord.

Paul speaks of those "better things" in Philippians 1:23, when he wrote: "For I am hard-pressed between the two, having a desire to depart and be with Christ, which is far better." Speaking of "better," he uses a superlative form of that word, which means *far, far, far* better.

The best is yet to come when we meet the Lord in heaven. Saying goodbye to Christopher has certainly not been "better" for me, for my wife, his brother, or for his wife. It has been the hardest thing I have ever had to do, and honestly, it breaks my heart even as I write these words. I want him with me so badly, but it is not to be.

But it *is* better, beyond all argument, for him.

So where is the Lord in our moments of tragedy, heartbreak, and anxiety? Where was He on July 24, 2008, a little after nine o'clock in the morning when my son died?

He was with me…comforting me in my moment of deepest anguish and sadness.

He was with Christopher…ushering him into the glory of heaven.

And He is still with both of us. In the same way, He will be with you in your good days and your bad days. He will be with you at the birth of a baby and the death of a loved one, who seems to be departing this life much, much too soon.

As the book of Hebrews assures us:

> God has said, "I will never, never fail you nor forsake you." That is why we can say without any doubt or fear, "The Lord is my Helper, and I am not afraid."[8]

David said, "Even though I walk through the valley of the shadow of death, I will fear no evil, for You are with me." And that is the great hope of every believer. We will never, never be alone. God will be with us through everything we face, and the best is yet to come when we meet Him in glory.

◌ Two ◌
What Do You Live For?

My wife Cathe was having a Bible study with Brittany, Christopher's wife, and I was on babysitting duty when we heard the news.

Christopher had been in a traffic accident, and he had not survived it.

Maybe you've been through an experience like this in your own life. If you haven't, it's difficult to describe to you. It's as though all the air has been sucked out of the room, and you can barely breathe.

There's such a sense of disbelief. Time stands still, and your mind refuses to accept the news as reality. And then, as the truth of it begins to take hold, you feel like you want to die yourself. Not to be morbid, but that's exactly how I felt: Like I wanted to die, so that the pain would stop and I could be reunited with Christopher.

I have never doubted for one moment that he went immediately into the presence of the Lord. It's just that I miss him. Terribly. Beyond my words to describe.

Topher was a handsome young man with a great sense of humor. The good-looking aspects came from his mother, and I suppose the funny part was from me. He was also a highly gifted graphic artist. People would say to me, "Well, he's an artist just like you. A chip off the old block." But that wasn't really true. Christopher truly *was* an artist. Compared to him, I am more of an advanced doodler.

But it's not only that I miss his talent or design work in our ministry right now. I just miss *him*. We were very close, and together all the time. And if we weren't together, we were on the phone with each other, or texting, or e-mailing. My last text to him was, "Where are you? Call me." He didn't respond.

But I know where he is now. He is in heaven in the presence of Jesus Christ along with everyone who has put his or her faith in Christ. That is the hope of the believer.

BELIEVING WHAT I HAVE TAUGHT

In my thirty-six years of pastoral ministry, I have talked about heaven countless times, and have given an untold number of messages on life after death. I have counseled scores of people who lost loved ones.

Somehow, I thought I knew a little bit about this subject. But when it happens to you, it's a whole new world. My desire to be in heaven is greater now than ever before, and heaven is more real to me now than at any time I can remember.

Why? Because I have an investment there now.

The Bible tells us that when a believer dies, he or she immediately enters God's presence. There is great glory in that place, fullness of joy at God's right hand, and pleasures forevermore.

That doesn't mean you stop missing your loved one. But it does mean that you know you will see them again.

People will often say, "I'm so sorry you lost your son." I know what they mean, and I appreciate it. But the truth is, I haven't "lost" my son because I know where he is, and I will join him one day. And all believers will join their loved ones one day soon.

> We tell you this directly from the Lord: We who are still living when the Lord returns will not meet him ahead of those who have died. For the Lord himself will come down from heaven with a commanding shout, with the voice of the archangel, and with the trumpet call of God. First, the Christians who have died will rise from their graves. Then, together with them, we who are still alive and remain on the earth will be caught up in the clouds to meet the Lord in the air. Then we will be with the Lord forever. (1 Thessalonians 4:15-17, NLT)

I saw a headline in a newspaper after my son's accident. It said: "Christopher Laurie dead." I have to tell you, that is a headline a father never wants to read. It was shattering.

But it's really not true. He's *not* dead, and I have the Lord's own word on that. Jesus said, "I am the resurrection and the life and he that believes in Me, though he were dead, yet shall he live."[9]

When you are a believer in Christ, you will never die.

No, I'm not in major denial here. I understand that this body ceases to function and we all have to face the reality of death. But the *real* you—your soul, your spirit—goes on to one of two places, heaven or hell.

People have asked me, "Are you angry at God?"

No, I'm not. How could I be mad at a God who forgave me of all of my sin? How could I be mad at a God who also forgave my son of his sins and holds him safely in His arms at this very moment?

People sometimes will say they are mad at God for certain setbacks or tragedies that have befallen them. The fact is, God ought to be mad at us for the way we have sinned against Him. Yet Scripture tells us God the Father poured His Holy wrath and anger on His only Son Jesus when He hung there on the cross. Jesus absorbed the wrath of God for each of us that deserved to face it for ourselves. Jesus came to pay a debt He did not owe because we owed a debt we could not pay.

No, I'm not mad at God.

But I am sad.

Very sad, and because of it I weep.

The Bible says, "There is a time to mourn," and I am mourning. I understand what the psalmist said when he said, "Day and night I have only had tears for food."[10] And I know that there will be more of that to come.

But at the same time, I am not as a person who has no hope. The Bible says we have hope as believers, no matter what the temporary circumstances of our lives might be. As I write these words, I am writing to myself, too. We all need to be reminded that life is short, death is inevitable, and eternity is real.

If there was some way I could have swapped places with

my son, believe me, I would have done that in a heartbeat. What if that had been possible? What if I could have done that? What would my last desire have been? I would have said to whomever stood up on the platform at the 2008 Harvest Crusade, "You preach the gospel, and bring many people to heaven as you can…I'm going home."

I bring that up because Christopher went to heaven only days before our crusade, and some wondered if I would still speak at the event. But the thought came to me that this is the one thing I must do, and I did. After all, Christopher did all the design for the posters, bumper stickers and website, as well as the design for the platform I stood on to preach the Gospel.

As I watched people flood forward on the field to make commitments to Christ at the close of the event each night, many of them touched by Christopher's story, I wondered if he could be watching this all from heaven.

I'll find that out when I get there, but I must say that it lifted me to see God work through this, the worst tragedy of my life.

What Do You Live For?

When you've had an encounter with death—a near-death experience of your own or the sudden passing of a loved one—it inevitably leads to a few essential questions.

What is life all about, anyway?

Why did they die, and not me?

Why am I even alive anyway—and what am I really living for?

In other words, what gets you out of bed in the morning? What gets your blood pumping? Is it an alarm clock or a calling that gets you up each and every day? Every one of us needs some motivating passion, some ideal, something that gives our lives purpose, that drives us on. Unfortunately some people don't know what they're living for. A poll was taken among the viewers of the Oprah Winfrey show some time ago. The question was asked, "What is your life's passion?" And seventy percent of the respondents had no idea!

Many people are merely enduring instead of enjoying their lives. Their favorite day of the week is "someday." Someday my ship will come in. Someday my prince will come. Someday it's all going to get better. Someday my life will change. A recent study revealed that ninety-four percent of the people surveyed were simply *enduring* the present, while waiting for something better to happen.

But here is what people don't plan on.

They don't plan on death.

And then never expect it to come around the corner unexpectedly.

Now when you're getting along in years as I am, death is at least in the back of your mind. You know that you have fewer years to live than you've lived already, and that death waits at the end…whenever that may be. But many younger people think they're invincible. Death happens to "other people." Cancer and heart attacks and fatal accidents happen to "someone else."

When you're young you tell yourself, "I don't have to even think about that for another fifty or sixty years." And that may be true. But death knocks at every door. The Bible says that each of us have an appointment with death.

> Just as man is destined to die once,
> and after that to face judgment....
> (Hebrews 9:27, NIV)

> To everything there is a season,
> A time for every purpose under heaven:
> A time to be born,
> And a time to die....
> (Ecclesiastes 3:1-2)

That "time to die" may come later than you expected. On the other hand, it may come much, much sooner.

Statisticians tell us that 3 people die every second, 180 every minute, and 11,000 every hour. That means that every day 250,000 people enter into eternity. The psalmist writes: "Teach us to number our days and recognize how few they are; help us to spend them as we should.... You have made my life no longer than the width of my hand. My entire lifetime is just a moment to you; at best, each of us is but a breath" (Psalms 90:12, TLB; 39:5, NLT).

Randy Alcorn, in his excellent book called *Heaven*[11], points out that Phillip of Macedon, the father of Alexander the Great, commissioned his servant to stand in his presence each and every day and repeat this statement:

"Phillip, you will die." In contrast, France's Louis XIV decreed that the word "death" could never be used in his presence. I'm afraid that most of us are more like Louis than Phillip, denying death and avoiding the discussion. The subject makes us uncomfortable and we don't want to think about it, let alone talk about it.

The truth is, only those who are prepared to die are really ready to live.

Maybe you're thinking, "This guy shouldn't be writing a book at this time of grief and mourning in his life. He should wait until he has a little more perspective."

That may be true. But I wanted to write this book in 'real time'. In other words, I write today as a grieving father who recently lost his firstborn son. But I also write as a believer in the promises of God.

As I write these words for you, they are also for me. I find that I need to "preach to myself" quite a bit these days.

Recently, I visited my son's grave. I have to be honest with you and tell you at this point in my life this is absolutely heartbreaking for me. Sometimes the hard reality of this all sets in like a massive weight. I think of the fact that my son's body is under that ground, and I can't speak with him and he can't speak to me. And I weep.

Then I "preach to myself."

As I sat on a little bench we put in next to where Christopher is buried and looked at the sunset, I said "Greg, your son is alive. In fact, he is more alive then he has ever been. Because Jesus said 'I am the resurrection and the life. He who believes in Me, though he may die yet shall he live. And whoever lives and believes in Me shall never die.'" (John 11:25-26)

My heart was a little lighter when I walked away, and my pain lifted just a little.

So, I write as a man with a broken heart to others, who also have broken hearts.

"FOR ME TO LIVE...."

In a dungeon in Rome, facing imminent execution, the apostle Paul wrote: "For to me, to live is Christ, and to die is gain. But if I live on in the flesh, this will mean fruit from my labor; yet what I shall choose I cannot tell. For I am hard-pressed between the two, having a desire to depart and be with Christ, which is far better. Nevertheless to remain in the flesh is more needful for you" (Philippians 1:21-24).

I love his statement, "For to me, to live is Christ."

But not everyone will love those words. Some will think a person who says, "To live is Christ" is out of his mind. They'll think, "This is a guy who's got his head in the clouds. He's out of touch with the real world." Or maybe, "This is a woman who's so heavenly minded she's not earthly good."

But that's not true. Far from it! Those who think of the next world do the most for this one. My concern is for people who are so earthly minded they're not heavenly good!

The apostle Paul loved life. And the simple fact is, no one loves life more than the Christian. We can enjoy it because we know it comes to us from the hand of a loving

God. That beautiful sunset…that's the signature of my Father who happens to be the Creator of all. That wonderful meal…the joy of love and marriage…the comfort of family and friends…the satisfaction of a hard day's work. All of these are beautiful gifts from the hand of our Father.

As James wrote:

> Whatever is good and perfect comes down to us from God our Father, who created all the lights in the heavens. He never changes or casts a shifting shadow. He chose to give birth to us by giving us his true word. And we, out of all creation, became his prized possession. (James 1:17-18, NLT)

But as blessed as we may be in this life, there is more… more than what we are experiencing on this earth. All the great things we do experience are just hints of heaven, of something better that will come for the man or the woman who has put faith in Jesus Christ.

C. S. Lewis made this statement: "All the things that ever deeply possessed your soul have been hints of heaven. Tantalizing glimpses, promises never quite fulfilled, echoes that died away just as they caught your ear." He went on to say, "If I find in myself a desire which no experience in this world can satisfy, the most probable explanation is I was made for another world."

Lewis concluded: "Earthly pleasures were never meant to satisfy, but to arouse, to suggest the real thing."[12]

There is another place, another time, another life. And

life on earth, be it 9 years or 90 years, is a nanosecond compared to eternity. Even so, it is here on this earth where we will decide where we will spend eternity. It is here on this planet that you decide between heaven and hell.

Now we love life as Christians. *To live is Christ.* Again, to quote C. S. Lewis, "Aim at heaven and you get earth thrown in. Aim at earth and you will get neither."

So here are Paul's words: "I have a desire to depart and be with Christ, which is better." I never really fully understood those words…until now. I read that statement from the apostle and say to myself, "Oh sure, I'd like to be in heaven. But then, I'm pretty happy here on earth, too." But when you have loved ones on the Other Side—and perhaps someone who has just recently made that journey—then the promise and hope of reuniting in that place brings great joy, and something to look forward to.

But we recognize that we have a job to do, and a task to fulfill here on earth. And that is why I am writing these words. I am a dying man speaking to dying men, and I'm saying that eternity is real. And you get to decide where you will spend it.

My son Christopher is in heaven. Not because he is my son, but because he believed in the Son of God and received Him into his life as Savior and Lord. That is why he is in heaven.

FILL IN THE BLANK

Paul says, "For me to live is Christ." If you were to fill in that blank, what would you say? For me to live is…what?

Some might say, "For me to live is to just live." In other

words, they just take it a day at a time. Life for them is mere existence. They don't have any philosophy to speak of, and don't like to contemplate the meaning of life. They just live for the moment, seeking to satisfy their desires, whatever they might be. This type of person is very uncomfortable with any discussion about life and its meaning. Their motto is, "Just live and let live."

Others would take it a step further and say, "For me to live is *pleasure*. For me to live is parties. To go clubbing. To have this experience, do this or that, try this recreational drug or that one." They live and die for those things.

I know that particular train of thought all too well. Been there, done that, and bought the t-shirt. Before I was a Christian, I experimented with drugs, partied, and all the rest of it. And I knew the answer to my hunger for "more" in life was not in those things. In fact, one of the things that brought me to Christ was a simple process of elimination. I knew life wasn't in this, and I knew it wasn't in that. And I began to search and wonder, "What is the meaning of life? What is the purpose of my existence?" It seemed to me that I had spent more time waiting for a good time than actually having a good time.

It was sort of like being at an amusement park. You wait for two hours for a ride that lasts a minute and a half. And that's the way it is with life before you come to Christ: you wait and wait to have your little pleasure. But the "fun" or excitement of that pleasure is short-lived at best, and usually has a lot of guilt attached to it.

Others might be nobler, saying... "Ah yes, for me to live is to acquire knowledge." And they will say, "I have multiple degrees. I have spent much time in the halls of academia and consider myself an educated and intelligent person." That's all well and good. But if your pursuit of knowledge fails to take God into account, you will end up empty.

The wisest man who ever lived was named Solomon. People came from all around the world to sit at his feet and glean his pearls of wisdom. Thousands of years ago, in the book of Ecclesiastes, Solomon wrote:

> "Look, I am wiser than any of the kings who ruled in Jerusalem before me. I have greater wisdom and knowledge than any of them." (Ecclesiastes 1:16, NLT)

But at the end of all his study and vast academic accomplishments, he concluded: "But I learned firsthand that pursuing all this is like chasing the wind. The greater my wisdom, the greater my grief. To increase knowledge only increases sorrow" (vv. 17-18, NLT).

In 1966, a year before he died, the brilliant physicist J. Robert Oppenheimer made this statement. "I am a complete failure." This man had been director of the Los Alamos Project, a research trained team that produced the atom bomb. He also served as the head of the Institute for Advanced Study at Princeton. Yet at the end of life, he looked back and declared it all meaningless. He said, "All of my accomplishments, they leave on my tongue the taste of ashes."

The real answer to life is Paul's answer. *To live is Christ.* No one who genuinely lives completely for Him will be disappointed.

It's an amazing thing to consider that the very man who wrote these words 'to live is Christ' was once known as the feared "Saul of Tarsus."

This was a man who had dedicated his life to hunting down Christians, putting them into prison and even having some of them put to death. It was the hard-hearted Saul who presided over the death of the first martyr of the Church, a courageous young man named Steven.

But one day Saul of Tarsus came face to face with the very one he was running from and fighting with—Jesus Christ.

> Jesus said to him, "Saul, Saul, why are you persecuting Me?" And Saul said, "Who are You Lord and what do You want me to do?"[13]

Saul later changed his name to Paul, and the world was a better place because of his conversion. From that moment on, Paul said, "For me now to live is Christ. I'm going to serve Him and follow Him to the end of my days."

Paul's full quote in Philippians 1 is: "For me to live is Christ, *and to die is gain."* Another translation says, "To die is better." How could anybody say such a thing? How could an individual in his or her right mind say that to die is better than living on this earth? It's because Paul understood what happens when a believer leaves this world.

> What shall I choose? I do not know! I am torn between

the two: I desire to depart and be with Christ, which is
better by far…" (Philippians 1:22-23, NIV)

The word he uses in this passage for "depart" is an interesting word that could be translated in several different
ways. One definition means "to strike the tent." In other
words, to break camp. You may or may not be a big fan
of tent camping, but I can tell you that my favorite part of
the whole experience is when we're getting ready to break
camp and leave! That's when I get excited. I can hardly
wait until I get home and get into that hot shower.

The same is true of going to the beach. I find that my
favorite times are when I arrive, and when I leave. When
I first get there, everything's good. I set up my chair, rub
on some suntan lotion, and break out a good book to
read, with the sound of waves breaking in the background.
Wonderful!

But after an hour or so, I'm sweating, covered with sand,
people pull up beach chairs right in front of me, and I begin
to lose interest.

Then I get excited because it's time to leave, and go home.

In this passage, Paul says, "I'm ready to break camp. I'm
ready to fold up the chair, I'm ready to leave this place and
move on. And let me tell you friends… *I can't wait.*"

This body that we're living is a lot like a tent. Just fabric
stretched over some poles with pegs attaching us to the
earth. It's not a permanent structure, and it wasn't meant
to last forever. The Bible says, "For we know that when
this earthly tent we live in is taken down (that is, when we

die and leave this earthly body), we will have a house in heaven, an eternal body made for us by God himself and not by human hands" (2 Corinthians 5:1, NLT).

That word "depart" Paul used in Philippians 1:23 could also be used to describe a prisoner being released from shackles. Ironically, when Paul made this statement he was actually chained up under house arrest in Rome. His chains were made of iron, but perhaps you're dealing with chains of a different sort: an addiction or vice of some kind. Whatever it is, Paul is saying that there's coming a day when I will be released from these shackles.

There is one additional way "depart" could be translated. The word was also used to describe untying a boat from its moorings…sort of like when you set sail.

We understandably feel great sadness when a loved one leaves us, and sometimes we feel sorry for that person. We say, "Oh, poor John. I wish he could be with us today."

But stop and think about it. Think about the port they have left, and the port they're heading for. If you stood on the wharf and said goodbye to someone sailing off in a leaky, rusty old freighter bound for Outer Siberia or Lower Slobovia, well, that would be pretty sad. But if you went down to the dock and saw that they were boarding a beautiful, gleaming new cruise ship destined for Tahiti, you might be more inclined to feel sorry for yourself instead! After all, you would be the one left standing on the shore, and your loved one would be on his or her way to great adventure and a beautiful destination.

And heaven, in the presence of Jesus Christ, is exactly as Paul describes it: "better by far." Why? Because heaven is infinitely better than life on earth.

In Revelation 7, the Bible says of those in heaven, "They will never again be hungry or thirsty; they will never be scorched by the heat of the sun. For the Lamb on the throne will be their Shepherd. He will lead them to springs of life-giving water" (vv. 16-17, NLT).

Why is heaven better than earth? It's better because we are moving from a tent to a mansion. The Bible compares heaven to a city, a garden, and a paradise. These are ideas that we can attempt to wrap our minds around. But then again, the majesty and beauty of heaven will always be difficult for a finite mind to grasp. The general idea, however, is that one day we will leave a broken-down shack with a leaky roof for a mansion far better than anything we could ever find on earth. There will be no more devil, no more temptation to sin, and we will be reunited with loved ones in the presence of Jesus Christ.

Here's the way the writer of the book of Hebrews describes it:

> You have come to Mount Zion, to the city of the living God, the heavenly Jerusalem, and to countless thousands of angels in a joyful gathering. You have come to the assembly of God's firstborn children, whose names are written in heaven. You have come to God himself, who is the judge over all things. You have come to the spirits of the righteous ones in heaven who have now

been made perfect. You have come to Jesus, the one who mediates the new covenant between God and people…. (Hebrews 12:22-24, NLT)

It sounds like a place where I'd like to be!

The reality of heaven is immediate after we leave this life. We will exhale our last lungful of earthly air and take the next breath of celestial air on the other side. Paul said, "I want to depart and be with Christ." Notice he didn't say, "I want to depart and go into a waiting room somewhere." Or, "Depart and go into a state of suspended animation or soul sleep." No. He said, "Depart and *be with Christ*." The Bible tells us that to be absent from the body is to be present with the Lord (see 2 Corinthians 5:6).

Heaven is better because when I get there, all of my questions will be answered. I heard about one woman's question for God. In an overly ambitious moment she had invited a lot of people to a dinner party. And she was just frazzled. But at the dinner table she thought it would be a good idea to ask her six-year-old daughter to say the blessing. So she said, "Sweetheart, why don't you say the blessing and pray a prayer over our meal."

"Well, Mommy," she replied, "I don't know what to say."

The mother said, "Just say what you always hear Mommy say." So the little girl prayed, *"Lord, why on earth did I invite all of these people to dinner?"*

We all have legitimate questions. Why did this happen? Why didn't that happen? And of course, I have mine, too. But the truth is, even if we had some of the most troubling questions in our hearts answered, we wouldn't be satisfied. The answers would only raise more questions! The Bible doesn't promise us a peace that necessarily gives understanding, but it promises a peace that *passes* human understanding (Philippians 4:7).

I received a letter from Warren Wiersbe, a prolific author and Bible teacher, after my son went to heaven. He said: "As God's children we live on promises, not on explanations. And you know as well as I do the promises of God." He went on to say, "When we arrive in heaven we will hear the explanations, accept them, and we will say, 'May God be glorified.'"

I have many questions in my heart in these days of grief and mourning, and I don't seem to have many answers. But here's what I know: I know my son, Christopher Laurie, is with the Lord. And I know one day all of my questions will be answered. In one paraphrase of 1 Corinthians 13, we read, "We don't yet see things clearly. We're squinting in a fog, peering through a mist" (v. 12, THE MESSAGE). The old King James version says, "For now we see through a glass, darkly."

It reminds me of a car with tinted windows. Someone drives by and you're straining to look through the glass. You're saying, "Who's in there?" That's how it is for us sometimes. We try to look at heaven. We try to figure out the big questions of life. And it's hard to make it out. Maybe we see a little silhouette, but we're not even sure about that.

But the Bible says we will one day be known even as we are known. To quote again from the Message: "It won't be long before the weather clears and the sun shines bright! We'll see it all then, see it all as clearly as God sees us, knowing him directly just as he knows us!" (1 Corinthians 13:12).

Most importantly, heaven is better than earth because Paul says, "I will be with Christ." And that is the greatest joy. Yes we will be reunited with our loved ones. But we will be with Jesus and we will never be separated from Him again.

But then again, you don't have to go to heaven to find Christ. In fact, it's the other way around: *You go to Christ to find heaven.*

Here is what I can say to you. Take the worst-case scenario of life: finding out that a loved one—maybe even your child—has been suddenly taken from this life. My family and I have just lived that terrible scenario, and I can say this. *God was there.* I have hit bottom, and it is sound. God is there. His Word is true. You don't have to be afraid; God will be with you no matter what you face in your life.

So often in this life we are crippled by our fears. What if this happens? What if that happens? Jesus says, "Don't be afraid; only believe." I'm not saying it's easy. But I am saying the Lord was there and He is there and will be there. For all of us. No matter what troubles we have.

What do you live for? Be honest now. If your answer is, "For me to live is money," then to die is to leave it all behind. If you say, "For me to live is fame," then to die is to be forgotten. If you say, "For me to live is power," then for you to die will be utter weakness. But if you say, "For me to live is Christ" then you will also be able to say, "To die is gain."

☙ THREE ❧
Songs in the Night

I remember the very first time I said the words, "Praise the Lord."

At the time, it seemed like an awkward phrase to utter. As a new Christian, I had noticed that all of my new friends said those words quite often. "*Praise the Lord. Praise the Lord.*"

So one day I consciously worked myself up to saying it, too. It wasn't easy, and I wasn't sure at all that it was going to sound natural, but I finally got it out, slipping it into the conversation.

"Praise the Lord," I said.

After I said it, however, it felt kind of good. So I said it again. "*Praise the Lord.*" And I meant it.

It's a wonderful thing when those words flow right out of your heart and through your lips. This is what you were created to say, what you were created to do. You were created to give glory to God. That is the highest use of your vocal chords, your lips, and your mouth: To give honor and glory to your Creator and Savior.

Maybe it's never dawned on you before, but God really *wants* to hear us give Him praise. Did you know that? It's true.

Let's use an analogy from marriage: Maybe you're a husband who loves his wife very much. I certainly hope you do. But do you *tell* her?

"Well, no," you might reply. "But I don't have to. She already knows that."

Does she? Are you sure?

"Well…yes. At least she ought to."

How does she know?

"Because I *think* those words all the time."

That's good, and very commendable. But you might consider verbalizing them! The simple act of speaking to your wife and saying, "I love you," will mean a lot to her. Maybe more than you might imagine.

Now God, in contrast to your wife, is a mind reader. He knows precisely what you are thinking and what's on your heart. If you think, "I really do love the Lord," He sees that thought. But He still wants to hear it. Hebrews 13:15 says, "Let us offer the sacrifice of praise to God continually, that is, the fruit of our lips, giving thanks to His name."

The "fruit of our lips" means saying words of honor and praise and thanksgiving with our voice. Why does He want you to say it when He already knows it? Because it is good for you to say it…and good for other ears to hear it. What's more, this passage in Hebrews makes clear that we should offer such praise to God whether we feel it or whether we *don't* feel it. We need to give God what He deserves, and what He deserves—now and forever—is glory. Psalm 29:2 says, "Give unto the LORD the glory due His name; worship the LORD in the beauty of holiness."

But far too often we're like those ten lepers in Luke 17 who called out loudly to Jesus for intervention in their trouble and trials. The Lord graciously heard their prayer, and healed all of them of the dreaded disease of leprosy. But as you may know, only one returned to give thanks. And Jesus said in response, "Didn't I heal ten men? Where are the other nine?" (v. 17).

We're often quick to ask God for help during times of crisis, but we tend to be very slow to offer God thanks after He steps in and helps us. Essentially we say, "Thanks, God. I'll check in with You at the next crisis."

But at least one of those lepers, realizing he had been healed, "with a loud voice glorified God, and fell down on his face at His feet, giving Him thanks" (v. 16). By the way, that phrase "loud voice" is translated from two Greek words from which we get our English words *megaphone*. He praised the Lord with his voice, and he pumped up the volume as he did.

Here are three quick takeaway truths I need to know about God that will help me in my thanksgiving to Him.

So Why Should I Praise God?

#1: Because He is in Control

As a believer in Christ, I must realize that God is in control of all the circumstances surrounding my life. *Nothing* escapes His attention. Sometimes we understand these circumstances—or think we do. At other times, these events make no sense to us at all, and leave us baffled and perplexed. We make our plans, yes, but God will always have His way. There's not a thing wrong with dreaming and thinking ahead and setting goals for tomorrow or for next month or next year; just remember that the Lord may change your plans, and it is His prerogative to do so. He, not you, is in control of your life, as Scripture makes clear.

> We can make our plans,
> but the LORD determines our steps.
> (Proverbs 16:9, NLT)

> O LORD, I know the way of man is not in himself;
> It is not in man who walks to direct his own steps.
> (Jeremiah 10:23)

> A man's steps are of the LORD;
> How then can a man understand his own way?
> (Proverbs 20:24)

We call this "divine providence," and that's a term that sounds pleasing to us. But it doesn't mean that bad things won't happen to good and even godly people. It does mean that even *when* bad things happen, God can bring good out of bad. Romans 8:28 reminds us that, "all things are working together for good to those that love God and are the called according to His purpose."

Many through the years have drawn hope and comfort from that promise. But here's what we sometimes fail to realize: *The "good" that God promises won't be fully realized until we get to heaven.* There are some things we can look at in life and say, "Well, that was really bad. No doubt about it. But now as I look back in retrospect, I can see the good that has come from it." But there are other times and other circumstances we endure in life where we may never be able to see anything remotely "good." At least outwardly. It's not until we get to the other side and see the Lord face to face that we will understand these things.

#2: Because God is good.

I must realize God loves me and is always looking out for my eternal benefit. In Paul's second letter to the Corinthians, he writes; "For our present troubles are small and won't last very long. Yet they produce for us a glory that vastly outweighs them and will last forever! So we don't look at the troubles we can see now; rather, we fix our gaze on things that cannot be seen. For the things we see now will soon be gone, but the things we cannot see will last forever" (2 Corinthians 4:17-18, NLT).

I would suggest to you that what we sometimes perceive as "good" could potentially be *bad*. And what we sometimes perceive as "bad" could potentially be *good*.

We think, for instance, that having perfect health and lots of money and influence would be unqualified "goods." Not necessarily! The fact is, what's good for one person won't always be good for another. Just look at how the lives of some people have fared after winning massive amounts of money in the lottery. After dreaming and hoping—and probably even praying—to win the big prize, some people who have actually collected on that fantasy have found themselves in a nightmare. As it turns out for so many, the "easy millions" have ended up permanently devastating their families and their lives. What could be perceived as the greatest thing that could happen to them has actually become a curse.

That's not true of everyone, of course. We all know people who have been blessed with affluence and handled it very wisely. The bottom line, however, is that it is God who determines these things. Sometimes the very situation that looks so depressing and heartbreaking to me today may ultimately be something very good for me in the days to come, because it changes who I am. It shakes me out of some deep, life-consuming ruts, and makes me more like Jesus. By the same token, sometimes what I might first regard as good can end up being very damaging, because it causes me to forget God and instead trust in myself.

#3: Because God is wiser than I am

My heavenly Father always deals with me for my best and for my eternal good. What are those people, events, or situations in my life that will result in my becoming more and more like Jesus? Bottom line...that's for the Father—in His love, goodness, and in His infinite wisdom—to sort out, not me. He knows best what tools to use on me as He shapes me to look more and more like His Son. I have one responsibility, and that is to glorify God with my life.

Acts 16 gives us a dark and gritty—but beautiful—story of two men who did just that.

A MISSION INTO THE DARK

Concerned for the new churches he had left behind in Asia Minor, the apostle Paul proposed a second missionary journey to revisit those congregations and check on their progress. Before launching out, Paul and Silas—possibly with input from the elders of the Antioch church—would have planned a careful itinerary.

But there was one small problem. God had a different game plan than the one they had come up with. The Holy Spirit actually stepped in to stop them from where they initially wanted to go.

We read in Acts 16: "Next Paul and Silas traveled through the area of Phrygia and Galatia, because the Holy Spirit had prevented them from preaching the word in the province of Asia at that time. Then coming to the borders of Mysia, they headed north for the province of Bithynia, but again the Spirit of Jesus did not allow them to go there" (vv. 6-7, NLT).

I find that turn of events fascinating.

The Holy Spirit—twice—kept them from ministering where they had planned to minister. The Bible doesn't tell us how He stopped them, but suffice it to say that God gave them a clear "no." And there was no mistaking God's red light for a green one!

Sometimes the Lord will do that with us. We have our plans, and we say, "Well, Lord, I think I should do thus and so." We've done our research, we've received good counsel, we've prayed about it, and we begin to move ahead. But then suddenly and unexpectedly the Lord closes the door.

How does He stop us? In many different ways. Sometimes it's through the warning of a respected friend, who will say, "You know, I really don't think you should be doing that." Sometimes it might be through a lack of peace in our lives, where we start to walk in a certain direction because the circumstances seem favorable, and yet…something just doesn't feel quite right. We have a lack of peace about it.

We are told in the book of Colossians that we should let the peace of God settle with finality all matters that arise in our mind.[14] And if you are starting to do something or go somewhere and you feel uneasy about it, or wonder if it really has the Lord's blessing, then you should learn to tune in and listen to that.

Sometimes it can be circumstantial. Something as simple as a car not starting. Or a door not opening. Or you're late for the flight. Or you come down with a virus. All your plans get set aside, because the Lord has said no, you're not going to do that right now.

Maybe you have had plans and dreams and God has said, "No. That is not what I had in mind for you. I want you to do something different."

You wanted to go into ministry, and instead God called you into business.

You wanted to go into business, and instead God called you into ministry.

You wanted to be married and God called you to be single.

You'd planned on staying single, but God brought someone into your life.

You hoped for a large family, and God gave you a small one.

These circumstances in which you find yourself may be very different from what you had wanted or visualized. But you need to understand that God has His purposes in these things.

So when they were thwarted from carrying out Plan A, Paul and Silas immediately shifted to Plan B, and went in a different direction. It began with a vision in the night, where a man from Macedonia called out to Paul, *"Come here and help us"* (See Acts 16:9-10).

In view of what would later happen to these two men, it's very significant that God clearly *called* them to Macedonia and to Philippi. Even though the path ahead of them would grow very dark, they had the assurance in their hearts that they were walking in God's plan and according to His desires.

So they made the journey to Philippi. Later, of course, Paul wrote an epistle to the believers called the book of Philippians, which has been such an encouragement to believers down through the centuries. Philippi was a Roman colony. When Rome conquered multiple territories they would set up colonies in various places. And though they were not close to Rome itself, they would be what we might describe as "a Rome away from Rome," if you will. Roman customs would be observed, and Roman law would be enforced.

Initially, things looked pretty good for this mission trip to Philippi. Paul and Silas started their evangelistic ministry, and a prominent businesswoman named Lydia responded to the gospel. After she and her whole household came to the Lord and were baptized, she invited the two missionaries to stay in her home, giving them what must have been a very comfortable base of operations. What a great start!

Before they were hardly out of the blocks, however, Satan stepped in and stirred up strong opposition to their message. You can read the details of that conflict in Acts 16:16-21. Suffice it to say that this is the way it will always happen. Whenever the gospel breaks new ground and begins to make some headway in a given city, town, school, neighborhood, or even an individual human heart, the devil is going to oppose it in some way, shape, or form. In Philippi, the enemy used the healing of a slave girl to spark trouble. But if it weren't that, it would have been something else. Satan could not allow the advance of the gospel into this pagan stronghold to go unchallenged. And he didn't.

Some troublemakers seized Paul and Silas (have you ever noticed how readily available people like these seem to be?) and started screaming, "The whole city is in an uproar because of these Jews!...They are teaching customs that are illegal for us Romans to practice." (vv. 20-21, NLT).

The text goes on to say that "a mob quickly formed against Paul and Silas, and the city officials ordered them stripped and beaten with wooden rods. They were severely beaten, and then they were thrown into prison. The jailer was ordered to make sure they didn't escape. So the jailer put them into the inner dungeon and clamped their feet in the stocks" (vv. 22-24, NLT).

Trouble? You'd better believe it.

Suffering? I don't think you and I could even begin to imagine what it would feel like to have our clothes ripped off in the town square and our backs bruised and bloodied by a mob wielding clubs. Adding insult to injury, the missionaries were thrown into a dungeon and had their legs jerked apart as far as they would go, and placed into stocks, resulting in even more excruciating pain.

But that's what makes the next verses shine so brightly.

> Around midnight Paul and Silas were praying and singing hymns to God, and the other prisoners were listening. Suddenly, there was a massive earthquake, and the prison was shaken to its foundations. All the doors immediately flew open, and the chains of every prisoner fell off! The jailer woke up to see the prison doors wide open. He assumed the prisoners had escaped, so he drew his sword to kill himself. But Paul shouted to him, "Stop! Don't kill yourself! We are all here!"

> The jailer called for lights and ran to the dungeon and fell down trembling before Paul and Silas. Then he brought them out and asked, "Sirs, what must I do to be saved?"

> They replied, "Believe in the Lord Jesus and you will be saved, along with everyone in your household." And

they shared the word of the Lord with him and with
all who lived in his household. Even at that hour of
the night, the jailer cared for them and washed their
wounds. Then he and everyone in his household were
immediately baptized. He brought them into his house
and set a meal before them, and he and his entire
household rejoiced because they all believed in God.
(vv. 25-34)

Archeologists believe they have discovered this dungeon
where Paul and Silas had been imprisoned. It was a small,
windowless room in the inner part of this Roman prison.
Needless to say, there were no sanitation facilities. We
might describe it as a hellhole.

What would you do if you ended up in a place like that?
What did Paul and Silas do? We read, "At midnight they
offered praises to God."

Now *this* was a sacrifice of praise.

Paul and Silas certainly had nothing to rejoice about in
their circumstances. If the Scripture had said that these
men groaned or wept or even complained over the injustice
in the night, we could certainly understand why! Frankly,
that's what most of us would have done. How natural it
would have been to curse the men who had beat them or
curse the jailer who had imprisoned them!

But no, that's not what we read in Acts 16. We read that
they sang hymns and praises to God.

Let's be honest here: When you're in terrible pain in
the dark and the middle of the night, it's not the easiest

moment to begin a worship service. Nevertheless, that's what Paul and Silas did. And that's what we can do, too—even when pain and sorrow are great.

But the Bible promises that God can give songs in the night. We're told in Psalm 42:8 (NLT): "But each day the Lord pours his unfailing love upon me, and through each night I sing his songs, praying to God who gives me life."

There's something about nighttime that can amplify our problems. Have you noticed that? When you're getting ready to go to sleep, your problems can suddenly crowd in on you and seem about ten times bigger and darker and more frightening than they really are.

All I can say to you regarding such nights is to pray, pray, pray. This is a time to commit heavy weights, burdens, and sorrows to the Lord…and over and over again, if necessary.

Sometimes I've become so weary on one of those long nights that I will say, "Lord, You know very well about all of these problems and worries. I'll tell You what…I'm going to go to sleep now, and I'm just going to let You worry about them for the rest of the night." Now of course I know that God doesn't "worry" about my problems at all. But the Bible clearly tells us to "Cast all your anxiety on him because he cares for you."[15] And, "Cast your burden on the LORD, and He shall sustain you; He shall never permit the righteous to be moved."[16]

God is in control of our lives whether it's daylight or deepest darkness, whether we are feeling on top of the world or like the world has just rolled over us like a bowling ball. In either case, in whatever our situation may be, we need to offer our thanksgiving to God.

That's what Paul and Silas did…and as it turned out, they had an audience.

An Audience in the Night

Verse 25 tells us that "the other prisoners were listening to them." The word that is used here for listening here could be translated "listening very, very carefully." Interestingly, the phrase could also be translated *listening for pleasure.*

When I hear a song on the radio that I really like, I feel a little lifting in my spirit, and I tune in with all my attention. I say to myself, "Oh man, I love this song!" And I listen for pure pleasure. Now nobody had any radios going in that horrible dungeon that dark night, but there *was* music, and it was coming from the very place where none of the other prisoners would have expected it to be coming from!

There was hymns praise drifting up from a dark little inner room, where two prisoners who had been unjustly charged and savagely beaten were offering their simple praise and thanksgiving to God.

So everyone was listening in, because they'd never heard anything like this before. I wonder if Paul and Silas were doing a little harmony on a couple of praise choruses. Probably not. It wasn't their singing that night that was so amazing, it was *where* and *when* they were singing.

You're not supposed to sing after you've been falsely accused and treated like dirt.

You're not supposed to rejoice when you're being tortured.

You're not supposed to praise God after everything conceivable has gone wrong.

But Paul and Silas broke all the expected rules. They sang out loud in a dark, oppressive, horrible place, and those who heard them could hardly believe their ears.

The fact is, people listen to you and me, too. You might not see them listening or realize they're listening, and yet they are. They're listening to us when things go well, and they're listening even more carefully when we're in the middle of troubles and trials. And they're saying to themselves, *These Christians are thankful to God when all the trees are leaning their way. I wonder what will happen when the storms come?*

What about when crisis hits you? What about when tragedy befalls you? How are you going to deal with it? When non-Christians see us giving praise to God under such circumstances, it opens up a door of ministry opportunity. And suddenly an audience will listen to what we have to say who would not have listened to us otherwise. This is one of the things that God can do through our pain and our suffering.

When you and I worship God on earth, we're somehow in tune with what's happening in heaven—because in heaven there's worship and praise going on 24/7. In Revelation 5:12, we read about a numberless multitude of angels and redeemed believers in heaven, "singing with a loud voice: 'Worthy is the Lamb who was slain to receive power and riches and wisdom, and strength and honor and glory and blessing!'"

I like to think about that heaven-earth connection that happens when we praise God and sing our songs in the night. I believe that when we bring our earthly praise into the courts of heaven, some of the beauty and glory of heaven splashes back down on us in return. And that's what was going on in that hellhole of a Philippian jail. A little bit of heaven was showing up in the very place where no one expected it could ever be.

God is looking for people to worship Him in this way. Remember that Jesus said to the woman at the well, "God is Spirit, and those who worship Him must worship in spirit and truth." And He also said that "the Father is seeking such to worship Him."[17]

And this worship has nothing whatsoever to do with the quality of your voice! You can be a great worshipper and not sing well at all. It's all about the attitude of your heart, and your willingness to glorify and honor God regardless of your circumstances. This is why we exist.

Something else happens when we worship God— whether corporately or alone—in spite of our life situation. As we do, we tend to discover a fresh perspective on our lives. When we first come to praise the Lord, our problems can sometimes seem so big they're almost overwhelming. That's because we have lost our perspective. And that is why David would say, "Magnify the Lord with me."[18]

When I magnify something, I see it up close. And when I praise God I see Him for who He is—which enables me to see my problems, for what *they* are.

Have you ever had a time where you've come into church, and you felt down in the dumps because you had problems X, Y, and Z happening in your life? And maybe after you gave yourself over to worship for a while and sat under the teaching of the Word, things began to look different to you. Why is that? The problems were still there, unchanged. X was still X, Y was still Y, and Z was still Z.

But somehow, after you spent time in the presence of the Lord worshiping Him, everything looked different to you. It's because you have seen the Lord in His glory; you've heard His Word, and the promise that it offers you. And when you walk out the door into the church parking lot, you've had a true perspective restored to you. You're seeing things in their proper balance again. As the psalmist Asaph wrote, "When tried to understand all this, it was oppressive to me till I entered the sanctuary of God; then I understood...."[19]

Let's be honest, sometimes you and I simply can't comprehend why certain things happen the way they do; it makes no sense to us, and it grieves our hearts. But when we gather together for worship, and see God for who He is, then we see our lives as we ought to see them once again. It's wonderful to remember that the all-powerful, all-knowing God of the universe loves me and is interested in what I am saying and what I am offering to Him.

"Always Be Full of Joy…"

Paul and Silas did praise the Lord in an hour of great pain and uncertainty, and it wasn't the last time they would do so! Later on Paul was arrested again, and imprisoned again. And in the midst of that imprisonment is when he wrote the book of Philippians, a New Testament letter that just resonates with joy and praise and thanksgiving to God.

If he had written the book of Philippians in an ivory tower or on a beautiful beach somewhere, it would have been one thing. But the words of this epistle are even more significant to us when we realize he wrote it from prison, not knowing whether he would live or die. And as he was wrapping up that remarkable letter, he penned the words, "Always be full of joy in the Lord. I say it again—rejoice! … Don't worry about anything; instead, pray about everything. Tell God what you need, and thank him for all he has done. Then you will experience God's peace, which exceeds anything we can understand. His peace will guard your hearts and minds as you live in Christ Jesus."[20]

You see, Paul isn't just passing along some sweet sentiments or pleasant thoughts. This is a command from God Himself. Paul is saying, "Remember. Rejoice in the Lord always. It's a command from God no matter what your circumstances are."

Any idiot can be happy when things are going reasonably well. But when you are facing adversity or sickness or hardship or death and then rejoice, that's obedience… that's faith…and that's very pleasing to the Lord.

The Bible doesn't say that Paul and Silas asked for anything in that dungeon. As far as we know, they didn't pray for deliverance—or even a good lawyer. They just glorified God and left the results in His hand.

In this particular situation, God chose to deliver His servants. He sent an earthquake that broke the prisoners' chains and shook open the prison doors. As a result of everything that happened that night, the jailer and his whole household received Christ, and tenderly cared for Paul and Silas's wounds. The next morning, they were allowed to walk free.

Years later, however, there would come another time when Paul would not walk free. In yet another Roman prison, he would be executed for his faith, and sent on home to heaven. (Which he knew very well would be the best thing that could ever happen to him.)

The point is, Paul and Silas were prepared to worship and praise God whether they were released or not, whether their circumstances changed or not. They sang songs in the night to the Lord, not because they believed it would be a ticket to freedom, but because they loved their Lord, and knew He was worthy of such praise…no matter what.

❧ FOUR ❧
The Inconsolable Longing

My little granddaughter Stella makes good use of the word "more" when she really likes something. Her favorite food, at present, is quesadillas. No matter what time of the day it is, she wants a quesadilla. Breakfast, lunch, or dinner.

Only she calls it a "dilla."

"Stella, what would you like to eat?"

"Dilla."

Being the great culinary expert that I am, I only know how to cook a couple of things—one of them being scrambled eggs (and the other microwave popcorn). But now I've had to expand my repertoire to do "dillas" for Stella. And usually when you give her one she will then say, "More."

It's the same when I read her a Bible story before bedtime. As soon as I've finished the story, she says, "More." So I read her another story, and at the end she says, "More." So I do another. "More." And another. "More." Sometimes I think we'll work our way through the whole Bible before we're done. *More, more, more.*

This is good. Stella wants more quesadillas, and more stories about Jesus. And I'm happy to supply those.

Sometimes, however, this desire for "more" can create problems for us—especially if we're craving more of the wrong things. I remember years ago when I tried my first Krispy Kreme doughnut. I happened to be in the South, where the franchise originated—and it was a long time before they opened up a shop on the West Coast.

Someone said to me, "Oh Greg, you've got to try a Krispy Kreme doughnut."

"A what?"

The name sounded so odd. How could a doughnut be crispy and creamy at the same time?

"Krispy Kremes. Greg, you've got to try one."

"I've had doughnuts before."

"Well, you've never had a doughnut like this."

So we walked into the little shop, and I had my first Krispy Kreme glazed doughnut, fresh and hot.

And I said, "More."

I actually made it to six. That is my all time record. But then of course after they make their way down to your stomach, you say, "No more! No more!"

Deep down inside, we're all like little Stella saying, "More." We always want a little bit more out of life. We want the newest. The latest. The freshest. The coolest. We want more. That's the way God has wired us. But here's the problem: As much as we live life, as much as we see and taste and experience, it always seems like it just isn't quite enough.

Do you know why that is? The Bible says that God has placed eternity in our hearts (see Ecclesiastes 3:11). In our heart of hearts, there is a recognition that this world is not going to be able to deliver on its promises.

ETERNITY IN OUR HEARTS

It's like that old song the church has been singing for decades… "This world is not my home, I'm just a passin' through…." The Bible says that we are citizens of another kingdom. When you put your faith in Jesus Christ, you become a citizen of heaven, because that is your real home. That's exactly what we're told in Philippians 3:20: "But we are citizens of heaven, where the Lord Jesus Christ lives. And we are eagerly waiting for him to return as our Savior" (NLT).

That is why we find ourselves with a deep-down longing for something this earth can never deliver. And that is also why we will always be a bit out of tune with this world and all it celebrates. Have you noticed? Sometimes the world will parade its toys and its so-called pleasures before you, and you'll find yourself saying deep down in your heart, "That just leaves me cold. That's not what I desire. That's not what I want at all." As followers of Jesus, we've tasted much, much better things than these, and we want something more.

C. S. Lewis described this awareness of something more out there, this desire we are pre-wired with, as "the inconsolable longing." He once said, "There have been times when I think we do not desire heaven, but more often than not I find myself wondering whether in our heart of hearts, we have ever desired anything else." He went on to say, "It is the secret signature of each soul, the incommunicable and unappeasable want. It is the inconsolable longing."[21]

I liken it to a homing instinct that God has placed inside some of his creatures. We all know that some animals have a mysterious ability to migrate or travel great distances to very specific locations. It's like a natural GPS system that God has placed inside of them. I've heard that dogs have that ability to some degree. Cats certainly have it.

I read a story about a cat named Clem that left home for years. After a few weeks, of course, his owners thought that Clem was no longer among the living—that maybe he'd been hit by a car or something equally dire. And then eight years later, there was a scratching at the door. They opened it, and a mangy cat walked in, jumped up on Clem's old favorite chair, and made himself at home, cleaning his paws just liked he'd made a quick trip around the block and back.

They thought, "Where did this cat come from? Why is he sitting on Clem's chair?" And then it dawned on them, "Could this be Clem the prodigal cat returned?" So they got out some old photos of Clem and sure enough, this crazy cat had come home after nearly a decade.

(Personally, I would have demanded an explanation from old Clem. Where on earth have you been?)

One of these days we'll be going home, too—home to a place we've never been. Since my son's departure, heaven has become more real to me than ever before. I find myself thinking about it more then I ever have.

Of course, I already knew a number of people who have gone on to heaven before me. My grandparents are there. My mom is there, and the father who adopted me. Friends I have known through the years are on the other side, now, and many familiar faces from our church.

But when Christopher died unexpectedly and went to heaven, I became far hungrier for knowledge of where he now lives. Initially, after his death, I would call his cell number, even though I know he would never answer again. I just wanted to hear the recording. I wanted to hear his voice again, even though it's not "him."

Yes, there are moments of peace and even joy; but as with anyone who has lost a loved one, mostly we're just sad.

But we also know this. God is with us. And there is blessedness in mourning. Who would have thought it possible? When we use the term "blessed" or "blessedness," we usually associate it with laughing and having fun. But you can also apply the term to the process of mourning. Jesus said, "Blessed are they that mourn, for they shall be comforted." Or, put it in another way, "Happy are the sad" (Matthew 5:4).

There are things you learn in this valley that you will not learn anywhere else. Now if we had our say-so in the matter we would not be here. But we *are* here. So we want to learn what we can learn.

What Helps…and What Doesn't

Sometimes people will see you in the days of grieving, and they will notice that you're not smiling, or even that you've been crying. And they'll think, perhaps, that you're not doing very well.

Well, what are you expecting? There is a place for mourning, a place for weeping, a place for grieving when someone you love has died.

So don't expect us to get over it quickly. You can't "get over" someone who has been a part of your life—in our case for thirty-three years. You don't just edit them out of the script. When you're at a table to eat, you notice that empty chair. That person was part of everything you did—and then they're suddenly just gone. Yes, you know they're alive in heaven, but they're not with you anymore. And that is where the sorrow comes in.

I was speaking with Dave Dravecky awhile back. And you may remember that Dave was a professional baseball player—a pitching ace for the San Francisco Giants—who tragically lost his arm and part of his shoulder through cancer. A cancer survivor, Dave has used this as a platform to bring hope and encouragement to many, many people. As we talked together, Dave told me about his experience with what he called "phantom pain." He described excruciating pain in the arm that was no longer there—the arm that was amputated years ago. "It's strange," he said, "but I feel that pain in my arm right now—as though the arm was still there."

Maybe that's not the best description of what I'm feeling regarding my son, but that's what comes to my mind. He's no longer with us, yet in the place where he once was there is an ache that's bone deep—an excruciating pain and sense of loss.

Grief is like a big ocean wave. I used to surf with my sons. Topher, as with his brother Jonathan, was an avid and accomplished surfer. When you're out there in the ocean waiting for a wave and see a really big one coming, you have to make a choice. You have to decide what you will do with that wave. If you don't take action to ride the wave, it can pick you up and slam you down into what we used to call the soup, or the whitewater. And when you're in that turbulent, angry water, you can quickly lose perspective, even losing the sense of "which way's up?" The other way to handle a large wave is to catch it, and ride it as best you can.

Sometimes you will encounter a grieving person who has managed to ride the waves for a while, and he's keeping his head above water. Then at other times, you will see him when he's been caught in the wave, crushed by its force, and seemingly lost all perspective.

So when you ask a grieving person "how are you?", he or she may find that difficult to answer. Maybe it would be better to simply say, "I'm praying for you," "I'm sorry," or "I love you."

Sometimes a person may want to talk about their grief. At other times, it's the last thing they want to do. *And sometimes the best thing you can do for someone who has lost someone is not to say anything at all.* Job's counselors had it right when they first came to see him and console him. For seven full days these friends didn't say a word, they simply sat with him in his grief. Everything began to fall apart when they started talking.

When you're mourning, you are vulnerable. Your guard

is down and you are ultra sensitive—sensitive to things that will help you and sensitive to things that can hurt you as well. So if you want to say something to a grieving person, pray that the Lord will give you the right words. And if you don't know what the right words are, just give that person a smile and don't speak at all. Just say a prayer for them and leave them alone.

Yes, the Bible does say, "A word fitly spoken is like apples of gold in settings of silver."[22] But by the same token, a word *unfitly* spoken can be very difficult to bear.

Sometimes people will say, "I know what you're going through."

Most likely, they *don't* know.

To be honest, I don't even know what my wife is going through as she mourns for our son, even though we're together all the time. Her grieving process is different than mine. I had a person come up to me and say, "I know what you're going through. My grandmother just died." With all due respect, though I am sorry for that individual's loss, the loss of a grandmother is not the same as the loss of a child.

As I already stated (and as hard as it may be), everyone's grandparents and even parents will eventually die. Unfortunately, this is the way life and death work. But children are not supposed to die before their parents. That is not the natural order.

One person said to me, "What doesn't kill you only makes you stronger."

Needless to say, that didn't help.

Someone else wrote to me, "God always picks His best flowers first."

That didn't help, either.

Another person said "Your son is in heaven, so you need to just get over it!"

Obviously this individual has never had someone close to them die.

Otherwise they would never make such a statement.

On the other hand, there have been many other things that people have said that have been very helpful. So I'm not making a hard and fast rule here that you shouldn't say anything to a grieving person.

I'm just saying, take care.

I spoke with a Christian couple that had two children die. After the death of their second child, someone said "Well, it must be easier now that you have had one already die."

Unbelievable. What an insensitive thing to say. Listen, it doesn't matter if you have ten children. If one of them dies, you will mourn for that child as deeply as if he or she were the only one. Each child is precious to you, just as each one of us is precious to the Lord.

Another couple I know whose daughter died unexpectedly actually had someone say to them, "I know how you feel, our dog just died!"

Needless to say, that should have never been said. Better to have never spoken!

Someone asked me the other day "Well, have things gotten back to *normal* yet?" I will admit, that statement hurt. I told that individual that things would never return to "normal" without my son Christopher, who was a vital part of my life for thirty-three years. There is a new kind of "normal" to which I must adapt, and I don't quite know what that is yet.

Others will ask when we will "recover" from our loss.

One person who lost three members of their family in a tragic car crash wrote, "We recover from broken limbs, not amputations. Catastrophic loss by definition precludes recovery. It will transform us or destroy us, but it will never leave us the same. There is no going back to the past, which is gone forever; only going ahead to the future, which is yet to be discovered."

I have found that to be a pretty accurate statement. I will not "recover" or "go back to normal," because that would imply going back to life the way it was before. Life will not be the same without my son. But God promises to each of us "a future and a hope" (Jeremiah 29:11). I am praying that whatever that future may hold, I will honor God in all I do.

People will sometimes ask the question, "Are you at peace with your son's death?"

At peace?

Of course not!

Don't ever ask someone that. We should never be at peace about anyone's death. Death is an enemy. The Bible says, "The last enemy that will be defeated is death." Having said that, God is a friend, and I am at peace *with Him*. So we trust the Lord. But no, we will never be at peace with this thing that we call death.

For the believer, however, death is not the end of the road. It's only a bend in the road…a path that Jesus Himself has walked. And because of what He accomplished on the cross for us, the grave is not an entrance to death but to life, because death has been swallowed up in victory.[23]

So how does a person make it through such a dark and difficult time?

I'll tell you what helps me: Thinking about heaven. The more I think about heaven, the better things often are.

THOUGHTS OF HEAVEN

As I have said, heaven is closer to me than it has ever been before.

Newsweek magazine did an article awhile back called, "Visions of Heaven." The magazine pointed out that 76 percent of Americans believe in heaven, and of those, 71 percent think it's an actual place. But after that, the agreement breaks down. The magazine says that 18 percent imagine heaven to look like a garden, 13 percent think it looks like a city, and 17 percent don't know. The article also said that even those who say they don't believe in heaven at all wish there was such a place.[24]

We need to know what God tells us about heaven…get a lay of the land, so to speak. After all, if you're planning on taking a trip somewhere, you do a little research first. Right? You know…you ask questions like: How should I dress? Where should I stay? Where is the good food? What do you do all day? What's it really like? Things like that.

In Colossians 3:1-2, the Bible says, "Since then, you have been raised with Christ, set your hearts on things above, where Christ is seated at the right hand of God. Set your minds on things above, not on earthly things" (NIV).

The term that Paul uses here for "set your minds" is an interesting word choice. In fact, it is a command, in the present tense, that speaks of a diligent act of single-minded investigation. So the phrase could be translated, "Keep seeking heaven."

Warren Wiersbe reminds us that for the Christian, heaven isn't simply a destination, it is a motivation.

So What is Heaven Like?

Heaven is a place

First of all, it is an actual place. It's not an "idea" or a "state of mind," it's a *location*, like New York City or Chicago or Paris. I don't mean heaven is similar to these places in particular, but it is an actual city we will go to one day. And, I might add, it is perfect city, without urban decay and crime.

In Hebrews 11:10, we're told that this city's architect and builder is God Himself. And then Hebrews 13:14 (NIV) says, "For here we do not have an enduring city, but we are looking for the city that is to come."

Now we know that cities have buildings, culture, art, music, parks, goods and services, and events. Will heaven have all of these things? We don't know. But we can certainly conclude that heaven will in no sense be *less* than what we experience here on earth—with the exception of all things harmful or evil.

Jesus said, "I am going there to prepare a place for you."[25]

We often think of heaven in sort of a mystical way, and our minds gravitate toward the Hollywood version, where people in filmy white robes float around on clouds with little halos over their head, and no one really does much of anything (except occasionally strum a harp).

How boring! That is certainly not the heaven of the Bible. The Bible uses a number of words to describe heaven. One word it uses is "paradise." In the gospels, we're told that Jesus was crucified between two thieves. When one of those thieves came to his senses in the last moments of life and put His faith in Jesus, he said, "Lord, remember me when You come into Your kingdom."

And Jesus replied, "Assuredly, I say to you, today you will be with Me in Paradise."[26]

The apostle Paul, who had the unique experience of dying, entering heaven, and returning again to earth said, "It was paradise,"[27] a word that describes the royal garden of a king.

Heaven is also described as a country. Hebrews 11:16 says, "They desire a better, that is a heavenly country. Therefore God is not ashamed to be called their God." Heaven is a country, a city, a garden, and a paradise.

So often we tend to think of heaven as surreal, and earth as real. In other words, our point of reference is earth.

"This is earth. This is real. And heaven? Well, who knows?"

In truth, it's the opposite! Heaven is what is real, earth is what is temporary. That is why C. S. Lewis described life on earth as "the shadowlands." Earth is only a pale version of heaven. Not the other way around.

In his book on heaven, Randy Alcorn points out that Moses was commanded by God to build a tabernacle like the one in heaven. And in Hebrews 8:5, we read that the priests in New Testament days served in a place of worship that was only a copy, a shadow of the real one in heaven. In fact, as Moses prepared to build the tabernacle, God gave him this warning. He said, "Make sure you make everything according to the design I have shown you here on this mountain."

God wanted to make it clear to Moses that the original was in heaven, the copy was on the earth.

To quote C. S. Lewis again: "The hills and valleys of heaven will be to those you now experience not as a copy but an original, nor as the substitute is to the genuine article, but as the flower to the root, or the diamond to the coal."[28]

As earthbound human beings, we tend to start with earth, and reason up toward heaven. What we ought to do is start with heaven, and reason down toward earth. Heaven is the real deal, the eternal dwelling place. Earth is the copy, the temporary dwelling place.

When you see that sunset or that panoramic view of God's finest expressed in nature, and the beauty just takes your breath away, remember that it is just glimpse of the real thing awaiting you in heaven.

Heaven is a place of sight and sound, not some mere "state of mind." The King James Version uses the word "heaven" 582 times in 550 different places. It seems clear that heaven is not a dream, but a reality. D. L. Moody said that, "Heaven is as much a place as Chicago. It is a destination, a locality." Heaven is a destination, a place of friends and family, feasting, and fellowship. It is a place of activities and worship.

Will we know each other?

People sometimes ask, "What will we know in heaven? Will we recognize each other?" As if we're going to forget everything or be walking around in a fuzzy cloud of semi-awareness!

Here is the truth: We will know *more*, not less in heaven then we know on earth. We will still love, but our love will be perfected. We will still think and remember, but our thoughts will be perfected, too. We certainly will know each other in heaven—and infinitely better than we knew each other on earth.

How do I know that?

In Matthew 17 we read the account of Jesus on the mountaintop with Peter, James, and John. In those moments when He was transfigured before them, with his face shining like the sun and his clothes white as the light, He was seen talking to both Moses and Elijah.

From the account, it's obvious that the disciples knew

it was Moses and Elijah, though they were never told that fact or introduced to them. I doubt these two visitors from heaven had little nametags on: "Hi. My name is Moses." Do you think Moses was standing with two stone tablets of the Ten Commandments under his arm, just to give them a little hint? I doubt that, but there was something about these two that was instantly recognizable.

The disciples *knew* Moses and Elijah. And when we have been changed and encounter one another on the other side, we will know, too. But I'd like to add just one thing. If you ever want to look me up in heaven, don't look for a bald guy. Look for a guy with lots and lots of hair. (Then again, perhaps we will *all* be bald in heaven, as we discover that this is part of the new glorified body!)

The Bible says, "Now I know in part; then I shall know fully, even as I am fully known" (1 Corinthians 13:12, NIV).

Think of the purest, highest, most ecstatic joy on earth, multiply it a thousand times, and you get a fleeting glimpse of heaven's euphoria. That is why David wrote, "In Your presence is fullness of joy; at Your right hand are pleasures forevermore" (Psalm 16:11).

We will be aware in heaven. More aware than we've ever been before.

The good news is there will be no more senior moments on the other side! I seem to be having problems these days remembering where I parked my car. It happens all the time. I'll park it, we'll go in wherever we are going, come out again, and I will say to my wife, "Where did I park the car?" She says, "I don't remember." So I walk around pressing my alarm button until I hear it.

As Erwin Lutzer said in his book, *One Minute After You Die*, "You will know more there. You will love more there. Your love for family and friends will be a stronger, sweeter, purer love. Death breaks ties on earth, but they will be renewed in heaven. Heaven is a perfecting of the highest moments of our present Christian experience."[29]

What will our new bodies be like?

You will have a new body in heaven. Listen to Paul's words to the Corinthians:

> In the same way, our earthly bodies which die and decay are different from the bodies we shall have when we come back to life again, for they will never die. The bodies we have now embarrass us, for they become sick and die; but they will be full of glory when we come back to life again. Yes, they are weak, dying bodies now, but when we live again they will be full of strength. They are just human bodies at death, but when they come back to life they will be superhuman bodies.
> (1 Corinthians 15:42-44, TLB)

If you were disabled on earth you will not be disabled in heaven. If your body was broken down through the ravages of age or disease on earth it will not be that case in heaven. There will be differences in our new bodies, but there will be similarities, too.

The Bible says that our resurrection bodies will resemble

the resurrection body of Christ. For we are told in 1 John 3:2, "Beloved, now we are children of God; and it has not yet been revealed what we shall be, but we know that when He is revealed, we shall be like Him, for we shall see Him as He is."

What were the differences between the resurrection body of Jesus and the body that was put to death on the cross? When He walked among us on this earth, He voluntarily exposed Himself to the limitations of humanity. So when He was out all day walking, He was tired. Just like everyone else, he got sleepy, thirsty, and hungry. In His resurrected body there were similarities to the old body, but major differences, too.

His disciples recognized Him, and yet…something in them wondered, "Is it really You, Lord?"

> Now as they said these things, Jesus Himself stood in the midst of them, and said to them, "Peace to you." But they were terrified and frightened, and supposed they had seen a spirit. And He said to them, "Why are you troubled? And why do doubts arise in your hearts? Behold My hands and My feet, that it is I Myself. Handle Me and see, for a spirit does not have flesh and bones as you see I have."

> When He had said this, He showed them His hands and His feet. But while they still did not believe for joy, and marveled, He said to them, "Have you any food here?" So they gave Him a piece of a broiled fish and some

honeycomb. And He took it and ate in their presence.
(Luke 24:36-43)

But then again, He could do things He never did in His old body. He would suddenly appear in a room without using a door. And we know He ascended to heaven, which makes me wonder…will we fly in heaven?

Have you ever had a dream about flying? I have. Many times as a matter of fact.

I don't know about your dreams of flying, but in my dreams it's not like I run, jump, and shoot off into the stratosphere like Superman. No, I just lift up from the earth, float, and cruise around, kind of lazy-like.

Jesus ascended through the air, higher and higher, until He disappeared from sight. Will we be able to move around like that in heaven in our new bodies? I don't know? Quite possibly. (I hope so!)

Do people in heaven know what's going on down here on earth?

This is important to you if you have a loved one who's gone on to heaven ahead of you. After all, you were connected to that individual; you walked with them, talked with them, and now they're gone. And you wonder, "Does he have any idea what's happening down here since they left?" Or maybe, "Can she see anything that's taking place on this planet that we're still living on?"

I believe people in heaven know a lot more about what is happening on earth than we may realize. Here are a few conclusions we may be able to draw from Scripture:

#1: *When people believe in Jesus on earth, it becomes public knowledge in heaven.*

Jesus said, "There will be more joy in heaven over one sinner who repents than over ninety-nine just persons who need no repentance" (Luke 15:7).

What an amazing verse! Right off the bat, we learn that just one individual who puts his or her faith in Jesus Christ causes a party to break out in heaven. The residents of heaven are aware of the fact that repentance—a change of heart—has taken place. In Luke 15:10, Jesus goes on to say "There is joy in the presence of the angels of God over one sinner who repents."

Note that it doesn't say that there is joy *among* the angels in heaven, it says "there is joy *in the presence* of the angels of God." The way I see it, that implies that maybe someone else is doing the rejoicing. Do the angels rejoice, too? I believe that they do. But could it be that the rejoicing ones Jesus refers to here in Luke 15 are those who have gone on before us, who are celebrating the salvation of a loved one? Maybe even a loved one they played a part in reaching! Is it possible in heaven we would be aware of people that came to faith because of our testimony or our witness? We can't say for sure. But it's interesting to consider.

Again, Randy Alcorn in his book *Heaven*, makes a point about the believer's awareness in heaven from Revelation 6:9-11. In that passage, we read a description of those in heaven who have been martyred for their faith during what we often call the Tribulation period in earth's final days.

> When He opened the fifth seal, I saw under the altar the souls of those who had been slain for the word of God and for the testimony which they held. And they cried with a loud voice, saying, "How long, O Lord, holy and true, until You judge and avenge our blood on those who dwell on the earth?" Then a white robe was given to each of them; and it was said to them that they should rest a little while longer, until both the number of their fellow servants and their brethren, who would be killed as they were, was completed.

So here are these tribulation martyrs who seem to understand what is happening on earth. They knew they had been killed for following Jesus while on earth, and this demonstrates direct continuity between our identity on earth and our identity in heaven. They are not different people, but the same people relocated. In other words, those who have gone on to heaven are still alive, and they're still themselves! We don't have to speak of our loved ones who have died in the past tense; we can speak of them in the present tense. They've just been relocated: They were on earth, but now they're in heaven.

Second, notice that they were aware of the passing of time. In verse 10 they say, "How long, O Lord, holy and true, until You judge and avenge our blood on those who dwell on the earth." They are aware that this is an injustice. Then someone told them they should rest "a little longer." So they are aware of the passing of time.

Third, note that there is a definite connection between the believers in heaven and those on earth. Those in heaven speak of their fellow servants and their brothers. Sometimes we hear it said that people in heaven have no idea what's going on back on earth. But these people certainly knew.

How much do they know? To what degree are they following events down here? The Bible doesn't really say. But these people are aware, they are concerned, and they mark the passing of time.

Now granted, this passage is speaking of a particular group of people—the martyrs of the tribulation period. But they are people just like us, and what is true of them could also be true of us or others who have gone before us.

Finally, people in heaven may be watching us right now and cheering us on. Consider these familiar words from the opening of Hebrews 12.

> Therefore we also, since we are surrounded by so great a cloud of witnesses, let us lay aside every weight, and the sin which so easily ensnares us, and let us run with endurance the race that is set before us,

The Living Bible paraphrases the passage like this:

> Since we have such a huge crowd of men of faith watching us from the grandstands, let us strip off anything that slows us down or holds us back, and especially those sins that wrap themselves so tightly around our

feet and trip us up; and let us run with patience the
particular race that God has set before us.

Now what "huge crowd" is this? What is this "great
cloud of witnesses?" One big hint is the fact that Hebrews
12 comes right after Hebrews 11! Hebrews 11 is a record of
the great men and women of faith who died serving God.
We sometimes refer to it as the "hall of faith." You read
about Abraham, Moses, Joseph, Gideon, Samson, David,
Rahab, Daniel, and the list goes on.

So who are the witnesses? One interpretation of this
passage names them simply as people of faith who have
gone before us, giving us a model to follow, so we might
live and exercise our faith as they did. Another way to look
at it is that these men and women aren't simply giving us a
template to follow, but they are actually observing us and
taking note of our progress in the faith. They are the cloud
of witnesses watching us, and cheering us on, if you will.

Is that the case? Are there heavenly grandstands where
people monitor the progress of loved ones living out their
lives on earth? It wouldn't surprise me at all, but I don't
know. But I do know this much: We are in the race of our
life on earth, and we don't know how long it will last. And
I know for certain that Jesus is watching me, turn for turn,
step for step.

My son Christopher was quite the runner. When he was
in elementary school, he ran cross-country, and became
pretty fast. We would go to his track meets as a family, and
cheer him on. As he got older he continued to run.

I had been a runner in school, too—really more of a sprinter. I wasn't very good at those long distance runs, but I could turn it on for short bursts and do pretty well. So every now and then, I would challenge Topher to a race. We did this a number of times through the years, and though he got faster as he grew older, I could still beat him every time.

My secret was that short burst of energy. I'd just push a little internal turbo button and I could take off pretty fast and leave him behind. I have to admit it always felt good to beat him. *Ahhh, old Dad can still beat his son. I guess I'm not over the hill yet!*

Then one day we were on a beach and I said, "Hey Christopher, do you want to race to that mark right up there?" (I knew the race totally favored me, because it was a short distance.) He said okay, he would race. And so we took off and he was right up with me. Then I hit the turbo button! And I hit it again! And nothing happened. Christopher went cruising on by me, and won the race. I couldn't believe it! Actually, I was proud of him and crest-fallen at the same time. "Way to go, son. You finally beat old Dad."

We are all together in this race called "life." In his last letter before making his own departure for heaven, Paul wrote: "The time of my death is near. I have fought the good fight, I have finished the race, and I have remained faithful. And now the prize awaits me—the crown of righteousness, which the Lord, the righteous Judge, will give me on the day of his return. And the prize is not just for me but for all who eagerly look forward to his appearing" (2 Timothy 4:6-8, NLT).

I had always assumed that I would finish my race before my sons, and that I would pass the baton on to them. But my son Christopher beat me again! Beat me to heaven! And now, in effect, he has passed the baton on to me, and I have to finish my race. We all have a course marked out for us and a race to run and to finish.[30] And we don't know how long this race is going to be; we never know when our lives will end. So we need to be ready, and we need to run our race well.

In the gospel of John, Jesus tells His men that the Master Gardener "prunes those branches that bear fruit for even larger crops. He has already tended you by pruning you back for greater strength and usefulness…Take care to live in me, and let me live in you" (John 15:2, 3, 4, TLB).

I have been pruned. My branch…my dear son….is gone. Yet my life goes on, and the Lord still desires much fruit from the years I have left to me.

When we were children we liked to hear fairy tales, because they would always end with the words, "And they lived happily ever after." That's what we all want. We want a happy, fulfilled life. The young girls thought, "One day my prince will come." In one of the old stories, the lady kisses a frog and it turns into a handsome prince. But sometimes in real life, it's the other way around. The prince turns into a frog. The dreams dissolve in disappointment.

That's the way it is for many of us. Life didn't deliver. *Earth* didn't deliver. It never will. Yes, you will have your moments of happiness, your seasons in the sunlight, those sweet moments of joy and peace. You will see some beautiful things, and life, for a time, will be good for you.

But none of us, no matter who we are, will escape those darker seasons, those days of sadness, despair, disappointment, and hurt. Earth can't deliver on its promises. But heaven can. And for the Christian, we truly will live happily ever after—in heaven, in the presence of our God.

But not until.

❧ FIVE ❧
A Choice of Eternities

In the Bible, we read King David's words just after the passing of his young son: "I will go to him, but he will not return to me" (2 Samuel 12:23, NIV). And David comforted himself with that thought.

My family and I have also found comfort in that truth. Christopher will not return to us, but someday we will go to him. In the same way, you too will eventually join your loved ones and friends who have died in the Lord, and wait for you on the Other Side.

For me, one of the best pictures in the whole Bible is in 1 Thessalonians 4, where Paul describes a future incredibly joyous meeting somewhere in the clouds.

> And now, dear brothers, I want you to know what happens to a Christian when he dies so that when it happens, you will not be full of sorrow, as those are who have no hope. For since we believe that Jesus died and then came back to life again, we can also believe that when Jesus returns, God will bring back with him all the Christians who have died.
>
> I can tell you this directly from the Lord: that we who are still living when the Lord returns will not rise to meet him ahead of those who are in their graves. For the Lord

himself will come down from heaven with a mighty shout and with the soul-stirring cry of the archangel and the great trumpet-call of God. And the believers who are dead will be the first to rise to meet the Lord. Then we who are still alive and remain on the earth will be caught up with them in the clouds to meet the Lord in the air and remain with him forever. So comfort and encourage each other with this news. (vv. 13-18, TLB)

If my son could speak to us right now, I'm sure he would say, "Eternity is real. Heaven is beyond your wildest dreams. And you need to believe the gospel so you can join me here."

Life comes and goes, whether you're in kindergarten or on assisted living. The Bible describes life like a little flower that opens up the sunlight in the morning and withers that very day before the sun goes down.[31]

James writes: "What is your life? It is even a vapor that appears for a little time and then vanishes away" (James 4:14). Moses said that our lives are like a story that has already been told.[32]

Here's the funny thing about it. When you're young, life seems to go so slow. It seemed like I was in first and second grade for about thirty years. Every day took forever. Then as you get a little bit older, the months go by quickly. Years go by quickly. *Decades* go by quickly.

When my two-year old granddaughter Stella hears the words, "Just a minute," she doesn't like it. She doesn't like to wait—not even for a minute. Sometimes she will even

cry to hear those words. But then the other day my daugh-
ter-in-law Brittany saw little Stella telling the dog, "Just a
minute."

"Just a minute" seems long to a child. But as you get
older, just a minute comes and goes. God is effectively
saying, "Just a minute, and you will be with Me in eternity,
reunited with your loved ones." That's how fast life can go
on earth.

We hate to face the fact that we are mere mortals, and
that our days our numbered. Why? Because long ago your
first parents, my first parents, Adam and Eve, rebelled
against God and ate of the forbidden fruit.

The Lord had said to them both, "Don't eat it." But Eve did
eat it, and gave some to Adam who ate, too. And in that bite
heard round the world, sin entered into the human race. Don't
be too hard on Adam and Eve, because if you or I had been
there, we would have done the same thing. Nevertheless, the
Bible tells us, "Therefore, just as through one man sin entered
the world, and death through sin, and thus death spread to all
men, because all sinned" (Romans 5:12).

Death is like a virus that affects everyone.

But here is the good news. Jesus Christ overcame death
at the cross of Calvary when He died for the sin of the
world. The Bible says, "For our dying bodies must be
transformed into bodies that will never die; our mortal
bodies must be transformed into immortal bodies. Then,
when our dying bodies have been transformed into bodies
that will never die, this Scripture will be fulfilled: 'Death is

swallowed up in victory. O death, where is your victory? O death, where is your sting?'" (1 Corinthians 15:53-55, NLT).

Christ defeated death!

Now, I'm not saying we don't die. But I am saying we don't have to be afraid of death, because the real you, the real me, is not the body we live in. I am not merely a body that has a soul, I am a living soul wrapped in a body. The real Greg, the real Christopher, the real you is a soul that lives inside of you. That is why when you see the body of a person you had known and loved, it doesn't even look like him or her anymore. Because the real person has moved on into eternity.

What we need so desperately to understand is that heaven is not the default destination of every person. You must *choose* to go there. For instance, you can't just get in your car and drive over to Disneyland and walk in. You have to buy the ticket first. You also have to get your ticket to go to heaven. But you can't buy it. In fact, you could never, ever afford it. The good news is that Jesus Christ bought your ticket to heaven when He shed His blood on the cross of Calvary. And He offers it as a free gift to you right now.

My son is in heaven. Why? Because he's a preacher's son? No. Because he became God's son. How do you become a son or a daughter of God? The Bible says, "But as many as received Him, to them He gave the right to become children of God, to those who believe in His name" (John 1:12).

You may be asking, "What do you mean, *receive* Him?"

Just this: there has to come a moment in your life where you say, "Jesus, I am sorry for my sin and turn from it. Come into my heart. Be my Savior. Be my Lord." I can't pray that prayer for you. You must make your own choice. But when you have made that decision, the Bible says that you will go to heaven when you die.

Yes, we will all have to die, but all of us will also live forever. Everyone! It doesn't matter if you are a believer, an agnostic, or an atheist. In effect, we are all immortal.

You say, "That's good news."

Not necessarily.

Let's say that I bought you a plane ticket to go on a year-long vacation, all expenses paid. You would say, "Greg, thanks. That's so great."

But wait. Hadn't you better find out your destination first? If it's some rocky, God-forsaken little island in the storm-wracked North Sea, you might not accept my generous offer. If, on the other hand, the destination were Hawaii or some other island paradise, you would gladly accept.

In the same way, the issue is not whether you will live forever, because you will. The question is, *where* will you live forever? According to the Bible there are only two options.

Heaven or hell.

The believer dies and immediately goes to heaven, but it is a different matter altogether for the nonbeliever. They too, are immortal. They too, live forever. What happens to a nonbeliever when they die? Short answer: They go to hell.

I take no pleasure in stating this, or even in using the word. I don't want anyone to go the place that the Bible describes as "the second death" and "outer darkness." More important, *God* doesn't want anyone to go there. God says, "As I live…I have no pleasure in the death of the wicked" (Ezekiel 33:11). And that is why He made such a radical sacrifice to save us from that horrible destination. He gave His Son.

I know a little bit about what it's like to have a son die. I know something about that pain. Jesus was thirty-three years old, in His prime, when He laid down His life for us. Imagine how the Father felt when He saw people laugh at His Son, spit in His face, rip off chunks of His beard, and smash a crown of thorns down on His head. Imagine the Father's grief when they took His Son, ripped His back wide open with a Roman cat o' nine tails, and nailed Him to a crude wooden cross. Imagine how the Father felt when all of the sin of the world past, present, and future, had to be poured on His Son, who was dying in your place and in mine.

I tell you, it hurt. But He did it because He loves you. Because He doesn't want you to end up in a place called hell.

Jesus Christ spoke more about hell than all the other preachers of the Bible put together. You might say, "I thought Jesus Christ was the very personification of love and compassion." Yes, He was that and more. And that is why He spoke so often about hell, and the consequences of rejecting God's eternal plan. Because He loves us so much,

He is so compassionate toward us, He doesn't want anyone to go there.

If you knew a highway bridge was out on a road over a huge ravine, wouldn't you warn your family, your friends—or strangers, for that matter—so they wouldn't go over the side to their death? Wanting them to avoid a terrible catastrophe, you would take action. And that's why I'm sharing this message with you. You can avoid the catastrophe of hell by believing in Jesus.

You know the word hell. We throw it around a lot. If a situation is particularly bad, we will say, "Oh, this thing is hellish." Sometimes a heedless, careless person might be referred to as "hell on wheels." Or if someone had a lot of fun, he might later brag, "We had a hell of a good time."

I actually had a guy come up to me after I delivered a message in church and say, "That was a hell of a message, pastor." I think he wanted to compliment me. It is funny how we use this word. People will tell others to "go to hell." And then pollsters will interview people and they will say they don't believe hell exists. How is it that you can tell someone to go to a place you don't believe is even there? The reason you even use the phrase is because deep down inside you know there is a hell.

We know it…and in a way we think there ought to be such a place, because of the terrible cruelties and injustices in this sinful world. Sometimes people who have been terribly wronged may console themselves by saying, "Well, they'll get theirs someday." What does it mean when you say something like that? It means you believe in some kind of final judgment, a place of punishment, and you know certain people who deserve to go there—people like Adolph Hitler or a mass murderer. You say, "Yes, there is a hell for a person like that."

What is hell like? Can we get a look at it? There is an interesting story Jesus told in the Bible about hell—something of a peek behind the scenes of eternity.

Jesus told the story in Luke 16.

"There was a certain rich man who was splendidly clothed in purple and fine linen and who lived each day in luxury. At his gate lay a poor man named Lazarus who was covered with sores. As Lazarus lay there longing for scraps from the rich man's table, the dogs would come and lick his open sores.

"Finally, the poor man died and was carried by the angels to be with Abraham. The rich man also died and was buried, and his soul went to the place of the dead. There, in torment, he saw Abraham in the far distance with Lazarus at his side.

"The rich man shouted, 'Father Abraham, have some pity! Send Lazarus over here to dip the tip of his finger in water and cool my tongue. I am in anguish in these flames.'

"But Abraham said to him, 'Son, remember that during your lifetime you had everything you wanted, and Lazarus had nothing. So now he is here being comforted, and you are in anguish. And besides, there is a great chasm separating us. No one can cross over to you from here, and no one can cross over to us from there.'

"Then the rich man said, 'Please, Father Abraham, at least send him to my father's home. For I have five brothers, and I want him to warn them so they don't end up in this place of torment.'

"But Abraham said, 'Moses and the prophets have warned them. Your brothers can read what they wrote.'

"The rich man replied, 'No, Father Abraham! But if someone is sent to them from the dead, then they will repent of their sins and turn to God.'

"But Abraham said, 'If they won't listen to Moses and the prophets, they won't listen even if someone rises from the dead.'" (Luke 16:19-31, NLT)

Here were two men who had been living on earth in close proximity to one another. And then they both passed away. One man was wealthy and had everything; the other was poor, who had nothing beyond the few pitiful rags that clothed his body. One died and experienced incredible relief and comfort; the other died and found himself in a place of torment and suffering.

This isn't a commentary on wealth. The rich man didn't go to judgment because he was rich; he went there because he cared nothing about God. In fact, he was possessed by his possessions. You can easily see that this guy lived in luxury. If he were among us today, no doubt he would live in a palatial estate perched high on a hill…plasmas on every wall…cars lining the driveway…all the bling and every new gadget and toy you could think of. You would think, "Man, that guy's really living a great life." This man Jesus spoke of was eating all the finest food and had all the luxuries. Everything a man would want.

Meanwhile, somewhere outside of this rich man's gate, was this beggar named Lazarus. He was so weak, the Bible says, he was lying down, and couldn't even sit up.

Now back in those days, they didn't use silverware or cutlery or chopsticks; they ate with their hands, and then wiped their greasy fingers off on pieces of bread, throwing it to the dogs. Jesus tells us that Lazarus would have loved to get a few pieces of that filthy bread, but apparently nobody offered.

And then both of these men died. We can well imagine that the wealthy man's passing made the front page, and that he had a huge public funeral, with all the dignitaries in attendance. Everybody would have talked about him.

I don't even know if anyone knew that Lazarus died except the street cleaners who carted his body off to a common grave…and the God of the universe, who dispatched angels to accompany him into heaven. The Bible just says "angels." But how many angels? It could have been as few as two, or as many as a legion. All we know is that the man who had been so lonely and suffered so much during his life on earth, received a royal escort and welcome into heaven.

But isn't it interesting? The only character with a name in this story was Lazarus. The wealthy guy mattered so little in the eternal scheme of things that the Bible doesn't even bother to give him the dignity of a name.

Both of these men went to the other side, and I venture to say that both of them were surprised by what they found there. He'd never imagined such comfort. Such beauty. Such health and vitality. Such happiness. The rich man was surprised to find himself in hell. How could it be? Why hadn't anyone told him?

Both of these men were fully conscious and aware on the other side.

The man in Jesus' story says, "I don't want my brothers to come to this place. I want someone to warn them." But he can do nothing about it. He has made his choice, it is eternal, and there is no turning back. He can't warn anyone, ever. You can't make a call from the other side. You can't send an email or a text message from eternity. Once in hell there is no way to cross the threshold over into heaven. You are there forever. It has been said, "Eternity to the godly is a day that has no sunset. Eternity to the wicked is a night that has no sunrise."

That goes against the popular conception that hell will be some kind of unrestrained, eternal party. But there will be no party, no joy, no light, no hope, and no companionship in that terrible place. Those who go there will be separated from God forever. And we have the word of Jesus Himself on that.

Many ask, "How could a God of love send someone to hell?" The truth is, He doesn't.

It's not like all good people go to heaven and bad people go to hell. If that were the case, *all* of us would be in hell. Because every one of us is bad—bad to the bone. We're all sinners: you, me, and everyone you know. We're not sinners because we sin, we sin because we are sinners. It comes naturally to us—all of us.

I won't get to heaven because "I've been good." People think, "Well, if I live a decent life, try to be nice to others, and care for the environment, then maybe I'll squeak through." No, good people don't end up in heaven, either. Because *no one* is good enough to meet the righteous requirements of a perfect God.

The Bible says God is light, and in Him is no darkness at all. And every sin we commit is rebellion against Him. There is no way we can fix this apart from the Lord Jesus, and grace—God's unmerited favor—that He extends to us because of His death on the cross. He paid the price for your sin. And if you will take that ticket, so to speak, which He bought for you at Calvary, you can know with absolute certainty you will go to heaven and not go to hell.

The big issue on that final day is not going to be a sin issue as much as it is going to be a *Son* issue. The question—the *only* relevant question—on that day will be one that God asks: "What did you do with My Son Jesus Christ, whom I sent to die on the cross for you?"

God has given us the way into heaven.

But it's up to us to embrace that way.

Here's the hard truth: If you end up in hell, it will be because you effectively sent yourself there. And you did it by rejecting His incredible offer of forgiveness. C. S. Lewis said, "No one will ever go to heaven deservingly and no one will ever go to hell unwillingly." If you end up there you have to practically climb over Jesus to do so. He is trying to stop you. He is warning you.

Every one of us is an immortal being, and will live forever. But the question—the greatest question of our lives—is: where? My son Christopher had his ticket. He was ready to meet the Lord, and because of that he is in heaven right now. Have you got your ticket? Do you know with certainty?

I heard the story of a Christian father who was terminally ill, and summoned his three sons—two of which were believers to his deathbed. To the two young men who had trusted Christ, he said, "Boys, goodbye. I will see you in the morning."

Greatly distressed, his third son said, "Dad, why didn't you say that to me? Why didn't you say that you will see me in the morning, too?"

The father sadly said, "Because son, you have not put your faith in Jesus Christ. And because of that my heart is broken, and I will never see you again." The son began to weep. "Dad, I don't want to be separated from you. I want to be saved. What do I do?" And he said, "Son, put your faith in Jesus Christ, and then one day our family will be complete in eternity." And that's what the boy did.

The fact is, you can be reunited with loved ones who have gone on to heaven, or you can be separated from them forever in hell. The Bible says, "Enter the narrow gate. For wide is the gate and broad is the road that leads to destruction, and many that enter through it. But small is the gate and narrow the road that leads to life, and only a few find it."[33] Broad is the way that leads to destruction, and many there are that go that way, but narrow is the way that leads to life and few there are that find it.

It's your choice.

∂ SIX ∂
"I Still Believe"

It's one thing to talk about suffering, do a word study on grief, write about grief, or preach about grief.

It's another thing altogether when you find yourself suddenly submerged in it, out in the deep end, way over your head.

As a pastor I have been with people who have lost children, and have walked through those unspeakably wrenching and agonizing times with them. In several instances, because I personally knew the children who died, I have entered into grief with these families. I can even remember thinking, *Man, this is about as close as anyone could be to this without experiencing it.*

But I was mistaken.

It wasn't close at all.

The truth is, those earlier vicarious experiences were a million miles away from what we have endured as a family following Christopher's abrupt departure for heaven.

My son and I were very, very close. It wasn't a distant relationship, and added to all the grief I'm already experiencing, I don't have to sit around saying, "He never knew how much I loved him."

Topher new very well how much I loved him. I told him so constantly and he said the same thing to me. Would I change the events on that day in July if I could somehow turn back the clock? Of course I would. Would I have died in his place, if such a thing were possible? In a heartbeat. Gladly.

But I wasn't given that choice. So I just said, "Lord, he is Yours. I dedicated him to you when he was a little boy, and I dedicate him back to You again."

Christopher wasn't perfect, by any means. He had his prodigal moments, and drove us to our knees a number of times through his life. But he also had a tender heart. And whenever he did something wrong as a little boy, he could never get away with it. He would always get caught. His little eyes would fill with tears, and he was so repentant and so sorry it would almost break your heart. And then he would go right out and get into some new kind of mischief.

But the Lord was working in his life, showing him what really mattered.

In the last few years of his life, he took all of his considerable talent, passion, and creative energy and just poured it into his relationship with God and His ministry for Christ. Right up until the end, he was using his gifts for God's glory. We were just marveling at what God was doing in his life. He couldn't have been in a better place spiritually.

Many have mourned with Cathe and me, and we have read your letters and emails. In past days, I can remember writing blog entries and having maybe two or three people respond. Several days after Christopher's accident, I looked at my site and there were 15,000 entries from people all around the world. And we have read many of those messages. My word to all of those who have written to us and prayed for us is simply this:

I still believe. God is real, and He is present. Our faith is true. The Lord is with me moment by moment, and He will be with you in your darkest hour, too. You don't have to be afraid.

A few days ago I was reading my Bible in the fourth chapter of 2 Timothy. As I read, it seemed to me that the apostle's words applied to both me and to Christopher. This letter from Paul to Timothy contains Paul's last recorded words before departing for heaven (courtesy of a Roman executioner). He said:

> Preach the word of God. Be prepared, whether the time is favorable or not. Patiently correct, rebuke, and encourage your people with good teaching.

> For a time is coming when people will no longer listen to sound and wholesome teaching. They will follow their own desires and will look for teachers who will tell them whatever their itching ears want to hear. They will reject the truth and chase after myths.

> But you should keep a clear mind in every situation. Don't be afraid of suffering for the Lord. Work at telling others the Good News, and fully carry out the ministry God has given you. (vv. 2-5, NLT)

Now as I was reading, I thought to myself, "That's *my* part." The Lord has called me to preach His Word, to encourage God's people with good teaching, and to pursue those priorities even when it seems like my world is coming unraveled all around me. As Paul said, "Preach…whether the time is favorable or not." I am not to be afraid of suffering, and I am to continue on with an even greater commitment, fully carrying out the ministry God has given me.

And then it seemed to me like the text began speaking about Christopher:

> As for me, my life has already been poured out as an offering to God. The time of my death is near. I have fought the good fight, I have finished the race, and I have remained faithful. And now the prize awaits me—the crown of righteousness, which the Lord, the righteous Judge, will give me on the day of his return. And the prize is not just for me but also for all who eagerly look forward to his appearing. (vv. 6-8, NLT)

My son's race has been completed, and he is now with the Lord.

I would give anything to have Christopher back, if only I could. I want to put my arms around him. I want to hear the timbre of his voice again, and there are things I want to say to him. All of those things will truly happen, in God's timing. I *will* see him again and hold him again and walk and talk with him again. But I will have to wait for a little while.

Heaven is closer to me now, and earth is less attractive. But I still have a task to do, and I want to do it.

When Christopher was a little boy, I was always spoiling him. I took him to toy stores all the time, and bought him toys for no special reason or occasion. (It used to drive Cathe crazy.) Looking back now, I realize I was trying to give him the childhood I never had.

I remember the time we went to a large toy store, back in the days when the whole Star Wars phenomenon first came out. Christopher and I were looking at all of those cool toys together, and I said, "Pick out something for yourself." He went to the lower shelf with the little inexpensive figurines, and started looking at them—really thinking about it for a long time.

And while he was looking down there on the lower shelf, I was looking three shelves up, checking out the big time hardware. "Look at these X-wing fighters. Look at that Millennium Falcon! The lights actually blink on that thing!"

I was thinking to myself, *I'll just get something to go with whatever he picks.* Finally he said, "How about this?" and handed me a little Han Solo action figure.

I said, "Okay, Topher. And how about the Millennium Falcon to go with it?"

"*Dad!*"

We came home with our toys, and my wife just rolled her eyes.

I loved to spoil Christopher. And after a few of these

trips to the toy store, he started to wise up. When I would say, "Pick out something for yourself," he would say, "You choose for me, Dad." Because he knew I always picked the bigger, better toys.

In the way I've told this story before, I've always said, we're like the little boy in this story, and God is our Father. And when we let Him choose for us, He will choose better than we could ever think of choosing.

Many years ago now, I gave my life, my future, my health, my family, and my eternal destiny into His keeping. I have said, "Father, You choose for me."

He has made His choice. Frankly, it is not the choice I would have made, but I have entrusted my son to Him. And I know Christopher is safe in His loving arms.

He has chosen well for Christopher. And as I write these words, my son could very well be saying, "Dad always chose what was good for me. But my heavenly Father has chosen best of all."

☙ SEVEN ☙
Our Times... In His Hands

Why do some die young, while others live long lives? We can come up with all of our fanciful ideas as to why God lets one live and takes another. I've heard them all regarding my own son. People will say things like, "Maybe God was saving him from something bad," or "It's just that God wanted another angel (and/or flower) in heaven." The list goes on.

I simply fall back on the fact that I will probably *never* know why. And even if I did know, I seriously doubt that I would understand.

One day, however, I will. As we've already noted in these pages, the Bible promises that in the life to come "I will know everything completely, just as God knows me now" (1 Corinthians 13:12, NLT).

So why does God take choice servants "before their time"?

It's a question many of God's people probably asked about Stephen, a godly, vibrant young man who became the first martyr of the early Church. In that case, we can make a pretty good guess as to why the Lord took him Home. God used that shocking murder to stir the believers who seemed to be locked into a comfortable "holy huddle" in Jerusalem.

Because of the wave of persecution against the Church

following Stephen's martyrdom, the believers fanned out in the known world. And so did the Gospel. Then the very man hunting them and the Church's chief antagonist ended up coming to Christ! I speak, of course, of the conversion of Saul of Tarsus, who became the great apostle Paul.

It was still a great tragedy that a man died so young and so unjustly, and many godly people wept and grieved over the news of what had happened to him. He had been a good man and a good friend, and he was missed!

But that raises the question again. Why does God allow torment for some and triumph for others?

No one can say this side of heaven. The Bible gives us the account of wicked King Herod who arrested and immediately executed the apostle James—brother of John, and a close personal friend of Jesus when He walked this earth.

And just like that, he was gone.

Herod, seeing this pleased the religious leaders who hated the Church, was delighted when Herod followed up James's execution with the arrest of Peter. It looked like the end for the former fisherman and Church leader, but the believers prayed, and God delivered Peter from his prison. He lived to preach another day. In fact, Bible scholars think Peter lived at least another twenty years before his own date with martyrdom.

But why did James die and Peter go free? It's hard to say. The fact is, life just doesn't make sense a great deal of the time. But God has His purposes that often remain a mystery to us.

When we say someone "died before his or her time," we are making a false assumption. What we are assuming is that there's an unwritten promise of a long life. We somehow think that everyone, in the words of Spock from Star Trek, is entitled to "Live long and prosper!"

But the Bible makes no such guarantees. The Bible tells us that our times are in His hands (Psalm 31:15). It also tells us, in the book of Acts that "after David had done the will of God in his own generation, he died and was buried" (Acts 13:36, NLT). In other words, when David's time was up, God said, "Come on home."

We really have nothing to say about the date of our birth, or our death. Then again, we have a lot to say about that space in the middle.

Moses wrote: "So teach us to number our days, that we may gain a heart of wisdom" (Psalm 90:12). To "number our days" means to "make the most of our time."

So, here's how it breaks down:

- Don't take any of your loved ones for granted.
- If there's someone who needs to hear you say, "I love you," DO IT NOW!
- If there's a change you need to make in your life, DO IT NOW!

Dave Freeman wrote a very popular book entitled, *100 Things to Do Before You Die*. In the book he offered this counsel: "This life is a short journey.... How can you make sure you fill it with the most fun and that you visit all the coolest places on earth before you pack those bags for the very last time?" He goes on to detail some ways to "really make life count" by doing things like attending the Academy Awards and running with the bulls in Pamplona, Spain.

The sad thing is that the author of this book died recently at the age of forty-seven, after hitting his head in a fall in his home. He had only accomplished half of the items on his list. According to a friend interviewed after the author's sudden death, Dave Freeman's mantra in life was: "You should live every day like it would be your last." The friend added, "There's not many people who do."

Life, however, is more than "visiting the coolest places" and "having the most fun." There is a place for adventure and hilarity, but life—real life—is about bringing glory to our Creator, learning His will, and following it.

That is the *one thing* we should all be doing.

To close things out in this little book, let's go back to the home of Mary and her sister Martha one last time. The Bible gives us an account of a time when Jesus stopped in at their home to visit. Martha wanted to make Jesus a gourmet feast and was working slavishly in the kitchen. She got so caught up and flustered by this effort that she stormed out to where Jesus was teaching in the other room and demanded that her sister—who had been sitting at His feet drinking in every word—come and assist her.

The fact of the matter is, there is a time for work, and there is a time to sit and listen to what God has to say. Mary understood that. So, seeing her frustration, Jesus said to Martha "Martha, dear Martha, you're fussing far too much and getting yourself worked up over nothing. One thing only is essential, and Mary has chosen it—it's the main course, and won't be taken from her" (Luke 10:41-42, THE MESSAGE).

"*Only one thing is essential,*" said Jesus. Mary understood that essential thing to be time with God, and glorifying Him with her life.

In the final analysis, it's not a matter of *if* you will die, but only *when*. So do what you need to do now, and then you can live with a clear conscience, ready to meet God at the time He appoints, whether it be today or eighty years from now.

My son Christopher was walking with and glorifying God when he was called home. I was proud of him then (and told him so), and I am proud of him now.

I hope you too have found that "one thing" in your life as well. For you were created to know and walk with God.

Do you want to go to heaven when you die?

Are you trying to fill a void in your life with the things this world has to offer?

Friend, you were created to know God. And you can come into a relationship with Him right now, just like I and countless others have done.

God is only a prayer away.

If you want Christ to come into your life right now to forgive you of your sin…if you want your guilt removed and have a fresh start in life…if you want to go to heaven when you die, you might pray the little prayer that follows. I did that years ago, and Christ came into my life.

> Lord Jesus, I know that I am a sinner. But I thank You for dying on the cross for my sins, and rising again from the dead. I turn from that sin now, and ask You to come into my life as Savior and Lord, as God and Friend. I choose to follow You from this day forward, through all the days of my life. Thank You for calling me and accepting me. In Jesus' name I pray, Amen.

Yes, it's a very simple prayer. But if you meant it, Jesus Christ has just come into your life. And now…welcome to the greatest life of all—the Christian life. I want to hear from you about your decision. At your request, I will send you a Bible at no charge. Please get in touch.

Greg@harvest.org.

Check out our ministry website,
www.harvest.org.

and my personal website,
www.greglaurie.com

and finally, a website that features my books.
www.allendavidbooks.com

God bless you, today and forever.
Greg Laurie

Notes:

1. THE MESSAGE
2. Job: A Man of Heroic Endurance (Great Lives from God's Word Series, Vol. 7) by Charles R. Swindoll
3. See Deuteronomy 29:29
4. The Living Bible
5. Isaiah 53:3,4, NLT
6. From the song by Tommy Walker, "He Knows My Name."
7. Read 1 Corinthians 15
8. Hebrews 13:5-6, TLB
9. John 11:25-26
10. Psalm 42:3, NLT
11. Alcorn, Randy, Heaven, Wheaton, Illinois: Tyndale House Publishers, 2004
12. Lewis, C. S.
13. See Acts 9
14. Colossians 3:15
15. 1 Peter 5:7, NIV
16. Psalm 55:22
17. John 4:24, 23
18. Psalm 34:3
19. Psalm 73:16-17, NIV
20. Philippians 4:4, 6-7, NLT
21. Lewis, C. S.
22. Proverbs 25:11
23. Marvelous truth! Please read 2 Corinthians 5:1-5
24. Newsweek Magazine
25. John 14:2, NIV
26. Luke 23:42, 43
27. Read 2 Corinthians 12:1-6, also Acts 14:19-20
28. Lewis, C. S.
29. Lutzer, Erwin. One Minute After You Die
30. See Hebrews 12:1-2
31. Psalm 90:5; 1 Peter 1:24
32. Psalm 90:9, KJV
33. Matthew 7:13-14, NIV

Other AllenDavid books published by Kerygma Publishing

Visit:

www.kerygmapublishing.com
www.allendavidbooks.com
www.harvest.org